INSTITUTIONAL ADJUSTMENT
A Challenge to a Changing Economy

INSTITUTIONAL
ADJUSTMENT

A Challenge to a Changing Economy

PAPERS READ AT A SYMPOSIUM SPONSORED
BY THE DEPARTMENT OF ECONOMICS
OF THE UNIVERSITY OF TEXAS

Edited by Carey C. Thompson

UNIVERSITY OF TEXAS PRESS, AUSTIN & LONDON

Library of Congress Catalog Card No. 66–15705
Copyright © 1967 University of Texas Press
Printed by the University of Texas Printing Division, Austin
Bound by Universal Bookbindery, Inc., San Antonio

INTRODUCTION

In 1964 a grant was made to the Department of Economics of The University of Texas from the Excellence Fund of the University for the purpose of presenting a conference on a theme of the Department's choice. The conference was held in Austin during April 29–May 1, 1965, and the current volume contains, in modified form, the papers there presented. This introduction proposes to sketch the circumstances surrounding the choice of theme and participants for the occasion.

The members of the Department readily reached agreement that the conference should concentrate on matters which have long been the concern of their distinguished associate, Clarence Ayres. While through the many years of his service at The University of Texas, more diversity of approach and orientation has existed among his departmental colleagues than outsiders have recognized—even outsiders in the economics profession—those colleagues have shared and still share a unanimous conviction that the work of Professor Ayres has been distinctive and highly significant. His thought and writings have been concerned with many aspects of economics and with matters beyond the traditional borders of the discipline, but his efforts have primarily centered on a study of the processes of and hindrances to change and growth. His work provides, we believe, not only the means toward a much clearer understanding of the nature of modern industrialized economies but also an enlightening approach to the problems of the less developed economies. While the difficulties of the stagnant or underdeveloped areas of the world have received enormous amounts of attention from economists in recent years, it seems accurate to say that the profession's efforts to explain economic backwardness and to offer effective programs for economic growth have been marked, at best, by only minor success.

Professor Ayres' concern with these matters was exhibited in many publications in the years before World War II, and in 1944 he pre-

sented a careful and extensive examination of the processes of economic change in *The Theory of Economic Progress.* These efforts
appeared before the profession in general recognized that the nature
and causes of growth, along with the obstacles thereto, merited far
more attention as objects for analysis and description than they had
thus far received. The long-delayed revival of interest in such matters
unfortunately has failed to take full account of the earlier insights
offered by Professor Ayres.

It seemed to us, therefore, most fitting that a conference sponsored
by this Department should direct its attention to further study of the
processes of economic change. The venture was seen as a method
by which Professor Ayres' work might be examined and extended,
both by himself and by colleagues familiar with his approach and
sympathetic to it. It was also viewed as a method of offering opportunity for an exchange of ideas with other scholars whose earlier
efforts had probed into the nature of institutional change and the
means for influencing these modifications.

The two of our departmental colleagues chosen to appear on the
program, along with Professor Ayres, were Forest G. Hill and Wen-
dell C. Gordon. Both have been familiar with the Ayresian approach
since pre-World War II days. Professor Hill's studies have been
most heavily concentrated on American economic history, with
special emphasis upon the effect of public policy on technological
change and scientific achievement. Professor Gordon's primary concern has been with the field of international economics, particularly
with respect to the Latin American countries.

In inviting participants from outside The University of Texas,
we were fortunate enough to obtain acceptance from each person
on our original preference list. Our interest in Kenneth H. Parsons,
of the Department of Agricultural Economics at the University of
Wisconsin, resulted from his efforts to apply and extend the work
of his teacher, John R. Commons, who is recognized as having been
one of the profound students of the history of economic and legal
institutions of the Anglo-American economy. During much of his
life Commons was an active participant, at various governmental
levels, in understanding and directing the processes of institutional
modification through private and public policy. Professor Parsons
has continued such efforts; in more recent years he has been involved
in these aspects of development in other parts of the world.

Gunnar Myrdal has moved from an early career as a Swedish

economist to activities which characterize him as no less than
an international social scientist. He has achieved an extraordinary
knowledge of a wide range of economies and the institutional con-
texts within which they operate—perhaps more than any man in
history. His study of the Negro in American society is only one of the
many perceptive analyses in which his talents have found an outlet.

Most of Morris Copeland's academic career has been spent at
Cornell University, but he has had long and varied experience in
many independent and government research assignments. His best
known work has been in the study of money flows in the U.S. economy, but he has also concerned himself with various other aspects
of market economies, such as the problem of full utilization of resources, the topic with which his conference paper deals. He served
as president of the American Economic Association in 1957.

Gardiner C. Means achieved distinction early in his career through
coauthorship of two studies which vastly enlarged the knowledge
of that extraordinary institution, the modern corporation—*The
Holding Company* (with James C. Bonbright) and *The Modern
Corporation and Private Property* (with A. A. Berle). He continued
these and other studies in the 1930's, largely in association with
various New Deal agencies, such as the National Resources Committee and the National Planning Board. His ideas on administered
pricing, social control of industry, and monetary matters have been
recognized as highly valuable contributions to the understanding
of the American economy; his influence has been truly immeasurable.

We felt it very desirable that one participant in the conference
should be from a discipline other than economics. The work done
by Wolfgang Friedmann, professor of law and director of international legal research at Columbia University, and his record and
the range of his interests were such that we believed him to be
an ideal representative of the outside discipline. In his academic
training and residence and in the nature of his research and teaching Professor Friedmann has long been involved in the type of study
which this conference was expected to embody. As author and
editor he has dealt with such phases of the law as legal theory, administrative law in foreign countries, legal aspects of foreign investments, the public corporation, joint international business ventures,
and the law as related to social change.

It should be noted that the details of conference planning and
administration were carried out under the direction of a depart-

mental committee consisting of Professors H. H. Liebhafsky (chairman), Forest G. Hill, and F. Ray Marshall.

The faithful and effective service of the departmental secretarial staff, Mrs. Bonnie Whittier, Mrs. Margaret Armstrong, Mrs. Sandra Morrison, and Mrs. Gwendolyn Vail, in execution of many duties connected with the conference is gratefully acknowledged.

Carey C. Thompson
The University of Texas

CONTENTS

C. E. AYRES

The Theory of
Institutional Adjustment

Before we begin discussing specific institutional adjustments it might be well to devote a few minutes to prophylactic exercises. If we would guard against error, then (as Professor Copeland would say) we must define our terms. What do we mean by adjustment? Do we mean a pragmatic, or instrumental, or operational response to opaque facts? And what do we mean by institutions? Do we mean those social arrangements which have become so institutionalized as no longer to be amenable to pragmatic revision? If such is our meaning, then our project is by definition a contradiction in terms and we might save ourselves trouble by realizing at once that it is futile to go farther. But since we do propose to go farther, it seems clear that we do not commit ourselves without reservation to such definitions as these. Nevertheless we need not reject them altogether. It may be that the process of institutionalization and the process of pragmatic adjustment are, in some sense and to some degree, mutually exclusive; and if so, our problem is to try to understand these processes, and especially the reasons for their polarization or mutual repulsion; and to try to determine the limits of these processes and hence the prospects for adjustment which may be implicit in the present situation.

It has long been my view, derived from Veblen and likewise from John Dewey, that the process of institutionalization is quite different from that of pragmatic adjustment. This difference has, in my opin-

ion, never been described more exactly or more eloquently than in
the opening sentences of Dewey's Gifford Lectures, *The Quest for
Certainty: A Study of the Relation of Knowledge and Action.*

Man who lives in a world of hazards is compelled to seek for security.
He has sought to attain it in two ways. One of them began with an attempt
to propitiate the powers which environ him and determine his destiny.
It expresses itself in supplication, sacrifice, ceremonial rite and magical cult.
In time these crude methods were largely displaced. The sacrifice of a
contrite heart was esteemed more pleasing than that of bulls and oxen; the
inner attitude of reverence and devotion more desirable than external
ceremonies. If man could not conquer destiny he could willingly ally
himself with it; putting his will, even in sore affliction, on the side of the
powers which dispense fortune, he could escape defeat and might triumph
in the midst of destruction.
    The other course is to invent arts and by their means turn the powers
of nature to account; man constructs a fortress out of the very conditions
and forces which threaten him. He builds shelters, weaves garments,
makes flame his friend instead of his enemy, and grows into all the complicated arts of associated living.

Through the ages man has followed both of these courses, a circumstance which might suggest that they are compatible and even
mutually complementary. Yet the fact is just the opposite. These
two quests are mutually exclusive. One can prevail only at the ex-
pense of the other, and the whole history of mankind is the history
of this conflict. Both Veblen and Dewey understood this and stated
it explicitly, Veblen perhaps even more pungently than Dewey. As
he said in a celebrated passage in *The Instinct of Workmanship,*

. . . history records more frequent and more spectacular instances of the
triumph of imbecile institutions over life and culture [that is, over Dewey's
"other course"] than of peoples who have by force of instinctive insight
saved themselves alive out of a desperately precarious institutional situation, such, for instance, as now faces the peoples of Christendom.

Nevertheless neither Veblen nor Dewey ever gave us a clear and
acceptable statement of the reason for this fateful stand-off, Dewey
because of his preoccupation with Kant and the theory of knowledge, and Veblen because he allowed himself to be misled, by Mc-
Dougall and others, into explaining everything in terms of contrary
instincts.
    If we now venture to offer a different and much simpler and more

conclusive explanation of the polarity of institutions and technology, it must be with a clear realization of the advantages of following after. A lot of water has flowed over the intellectual dam. We know a great deal more about the natural history of institutions as well as about the history of science and technology than the Veblen-Dewey generation did, and it would be sad indeed if we could not see quite easily something that still remained obscure to Veblen's generation.

That growth is inherent in science-and-technology is now generally understood. It is so not because of any particular instinctive proclivity of man (other than general intelligence and restless fingers) but rather because of the nature of the process. All discoveries result from putting together previous discoveries, and all inventions result from putting together previous inventions. Inventions likewise lead to discoveries, and discoveries to inventions. It is of course human intelligence and skill that put things together. But the human element is constant through the ages, whereas the backlog of knowledge, skill, instruments, tools, and materials is constantly growing. The greatest genius who ever lived could not have measured the velocity of light or constructed a bevatron or spanned New York harbor in Magdalenian times; whereas today it is a commonplace of the scientific rat-race that if an American doesn't do it, a Russian will.

Clearly the reason for the bewildering rate at which science-and-technology has been advancing in the most recent years is not to be found in the prodigious hypertrophy of any supposed instinct of workmanship or of idle curiosity. It is the unprecedented proliferation of tools and materials of all kinds—intellectual as well as physical—that largely explains the rate of the advance just as the reverse condition largely explains the appalling time span of the old stone age.

Largely, but not altogether: for we have also to reckon with the inhibitory force of totem and taboo. Here too we can dispense with instinct, but not with culture. By what strange amalgam of emotion and intelligence man first began stocking his world with supernatural forces and imaginary beings we do not know. But we do know how superstitions and taboos have been transmitted. They have been transmitted by community indoctrination: a process of emotional conditioning begun in earliest childhood and continued throughout life.

This process is inherently static. Just as change is implicit in sci-ence-and-technology, what is implicit in the institutionalizing proc-ess is no-change. The past does not change, and institutionalization is commitment to the past. Mores derive their sanction from the past. Caste, in whatever form, derives its authority—or lack of it—from the past, which is embalmed in tribal legends. Ceremonialism, which Veblen regarded as the antithesis of workmanship, is an emanation of the past. Indeed, a ceremony is virtually by definition a re-enactment of the legendary past. Thus the whole process of institutionalization in all its aspects is past-oriented, and therefore change-resistant.

This means that wherever and whenever discoveries and inven-tions are permitted to occur, not only has human ingenuity put previously existing tools, materials, and ideas together to create nov-elty; but also some gap, some weakness, or some limitation of the prevailing institutional system must have permitted the deviation in question to occur and to persist.

Coming from me, all this must seem a twice-told tale. But I have a reason for telling it again. Just recently it has come over me, with something like the shock of discovery, that an organizational revo-lution may now be going on, in consequence of which the whole meaning of the process of institutional adjustment may be under-going fundamental change. This insight (or hunch), like all others, is a result of putting old stuff together in a new way. Consequently I will have to try your patience by rehearsing the old stuff a few minutes more.

For a good many years I have been emphasizing the interrelated-ness of the different aspects of the ceremonial complex. The cere-monies re-enact the legends; the legends rationalize the mores; the mores prescribe the behavior appropriate to rank; rank is the out-ward symbol of inner "mana" (mystic potency), or lack of it; and all are inculcated in each individual member of a community by emotional conditioning which is begun in earliest childhood and continues throughout life. I am extremely leery of set formulas, and so have always tried to avoid putting these items in any fixed order or pattern. But recently it has seemed to me that whereas rank, conventions, legends, and ceremonials are explicit social patterns, emotional conditioning is an all-embracing process, and supernat-uralism is a state of mind that suffuses everything.

There is a reason for this. Supernatural belief and emotional conditioning are obverse and reverse of each other. We do not know how supernaturalism originated, doubtless hundreds of thousands of years ago; but those who attribute supernaturalism to ignorance of natural phenomena are almost certainly wrong. Ignorance is a necessary but not a sufficient cause. The real affinity is almost certainly between the emotional susceptibility which mankind shares with other animals and the unique imaginative powers of the human mind. Not only do the more dramatic manifestations of natural forces, such as a severe thunderstorm, cause man to cringe in terror, as other animals do: man is able to imagine that thunderbolts are malevolently hurled by some vast but sentient Being; and he is able to verbalize such fantasies and pass them down from generation to groveling generation.

In this fateful combination the emotions seem to validate the beliefs, and the beliefs seem to stem directly from the emotions. This conjunction is what prompts people to speak of scientists as "coldly logical." As persons, scientists are of course just as emotional as anybody else. The point is not that scientists are cold but rather that their experimentation and reasoning are nonemotional, in contrast to supernatural beliefs the very transmission of which from mother to tender child, or from shaman to pubescent initiate, is a most explicitly emotional experience. In this experience the induced emotions and the supernatural beliefs which induce them are polarized, so to speak. Emotion without belief is functionless, and belief without emotion is inoperative. But supernaturalism *cum* emotional conditioning is what maintains all institutionalized social systems. It is as though myths, rites, mores, and status were structurally patterned, like building stones, to fit each other's contours, whereas supernaturalism and emotional conditioning are polarized, like an electric current which passes through the whole structure causing its parts to cohere indivisibly.

This is only a figure of speech. But the reality—the unique coherence of what anthropologists call the nonmaterial culture—is a fact. Indeed, I suspect that the anthropological doctrine known as "functionalism" is largely a projection of the coherence of these aspects of the institutionalizing process. If I have neglected it in the past, that may have been, in part at least, because of my obsession with the past-binding function of established institutions. But, as I now realize, what is significant is not only the sanction of the past but the degree of intensity of that obsession; and what now brings the coherence, or stickiness, of social systems into focus is long and continuing reflection on the extraordinary flux of Western civilization.

That Western development somehow broke the crust of ancient society has long been evident. How many circumstances combined to make this possible we do not know. I have argued, and am still convinced, that the location of this development not in a center of ancient culture but on what had not long earlier been a frontier outpost had something to do with it. So did the then recent derivation of the European peoples from wandering barbarian tribes. So, of course, did the severance of western Europe from ancient Mediterranean empire and, subsequently, its successful repulsion of Islam. At all events, for whatever reasons, the institutional crust of western Europe seems to have been uniquely thin and brittle and therefore permissive of revolutionary change.

The efficient cause of this revolution was of course technological: a unique series of discoveries and inventions which began far back in the so-called Dark Ages and has continued without break ever since. The circumstances by which these discoveries and inventions came about make a fascinating study, and it may be that my preoccupation in former years with this side of the picture was another reason for my failure to appreciate the importance of institutional coherence and the consequent effect of the scientific-technological revolution.

That effect is the point of focus of this paper. For if it is true that institutional resistance to change is to any considerable degree a function of what I have called institutional coherence, then it must be true that any short-circuiting of the current of emotional conditioning to supernaturalism will in effect short-circuit the whole institutionalizing process. That, I am now convinced, is just what has been going on.

Modern civilization has been undergoing de-institutionalization throughout modern times. The process has of course been a relatively gradual one, largely unperceived and wholly unintended, since it has been a function of technological progress and the growth of natural knowledge. Neither technological invention nor scientific discovery has been motivated by ideological disaffection. And yet the net effect over the past five centuries or so has been the virtually total demythologization of Western culture. The objective of every inventor is simply to construct a better mousetrap, and the objective of every scientist is simply to know a little more about mice. To both of them the outbreak of fresh salvos in the perpetual "warfare of science and religion" comes as an unwelcome surprise.

Hence the history of science-and-technology provides virtually no clue to the process of demythologization, let alone the de-institutionalization which is our present concern. Scientists identify the great moments in history in terms of strategic breakthroughs in their own particular disciplines, not in terms of the impact of science on our commmon culture. This was well illustrated not long ago by C. P. Snow, now Lord Snow. By way of illustrating the abyss of mutual ignorance which divides "the two cultures," scientific and humane, he exclaimed over how few nonscientists understand the second law of thermodynamics; and in this connection he declared that understanding it means nothing less than mastery of a series of equations in mathematical physics. In short, Lord Snow seems to attribute his abyss wholly to the scientific ignorance of nonscientists. And yet notwithstanding his literary career, he himself seems to exemplify the cultural ignorance of scientists, or their institutional neutrality. Why, after all, should anybody other than a physicist even know that there is a second law of thermodynamics? The answer does indeed concern us all. But it does not appear in any equation. As Lord Snow must know, the second law of thermodynamics in effect sounds the death knell of the human "soul." Like La Place's telescope, which swept the skies but found no trace of heaven, the second law of thermodynamics sweeps the universe and finds nothing but matter and energy. That is its cultural meaning.

It is meanings such as this which have given significance to the Copernican revolution and the Darwinian revolution, and perhaps the Freudian revolution. Without presuming to say what discoveries by what scientists have contributed most to the development of their respective disciplines, we can more or less definitely identify the institutional crises through which Western civilization has passed; and, however arbitrarily, we can attach names to these events. Indeed, in the cases of Copernicus and Darwin we have already done so. As a refutation of the Ptolemaic system the actual computations of Nicolaus Copernicus may have been far from definitive, as indeed I am told they were. Nevertheless he pioneered the secularization of the universe, and his name has therefore become inseparably attached to the first great step in the demythologization of Western culture.

In like manner the name of Darwin has been attached to the second great step: the secularization of the human species. In this case there is no question of the respect in which this great discoverer is held by his professional colleagues. The only question is with regard to his intent. What he sought to establish was the unity of all living things. But the whole world "got the message." As Clarence Day put it many years ago, it makes a good deal of difference whether we regard ourselves as slightly fallen angels or as super-apes. Whether or not he found this eminence comfortable (and apparently he did not), Charles Darwin has inevitably become not merely a hero of science but also the symbol of a vast cultural revolution.

I have given my third revolution the name of Sigmund Freud, although his name has not as yet been identified with such a revolution, and may never be. Nevertheless, by whatever name it may eventually be called, another such cultural revolution has been going on, and in an area in which he is the most eminent pioneer. This is the revolution in the emotional outlook of the Western peoples. Throughout the ages man has always been at the mercy of his feelings, and not alone in the sense of being a victim of his overpowering rages and debilitating sorrows. Emotion and superstition have always been linked. Not only do superstitions arouse emotions: the very potency of the feelings so aroused seem to validate the superstitions. This is especially true of the phenomena of trance states and even dreams, in which the dreamer seems to leave his body, to visit distant parts, and to move backward in time, or even forward. Nearly a century ago Sir Edward Tyler argued that dreams and similar trance states were the primordial source of all superstition. Doubtless that is not the whole story, but it is a significant chapter; and it is this linkage of psychopathology and superstition that gives especial significance to the book that made Freud famous: *The Interpretation of Dreams*. We do not now accept all of Freud's interpretations. But the linkage of superstition to common human experience has now been broken. All literate people now recognize that dreams and trances are evidence of nothing but the dreamer's previous experiences. They do not "prove" that the human "spirit" leaves the body, or exists after death, or indulges in bizarre adventures.

But perhaps Freud's greatest achievement, to which a host of his successors have contributed, has been bringing home to us the importance of the emotional experiences of childhood, and especially of earliest childhood. This process is the key to understanding the emotional intensity with which various peoples hold their various beliefs and adhere to their traditional ways of life. That is why so many cultural anthropologists have become students of psychopathology, and even practitioners of psychoanalysis.

But it is the foundation stone of modern psychopathology that getting the root cause of an emotional seizure out into the open of full consciousness means exorcizing it. This is what is now happening to Western civilization. Copernicus uprooted one superstition, and Darwin uprooted another. But modern psychopathology has laid bare and shriveled up the root cause of superstition itself.

This is truly cataclysmic. If it is true, as I am now convinced it is, that the myths, ceremonies, mores, and status systems which make up the institutional systems of all peoples are themselves welded together and shackled upon their peoples by a community-wide process of emotional conditioning to supernaturalism, then the short-circuiting of that welding current, which is the inevitable consequence of technological progress and its accompaniment of intellectual sophistication, means that the whole institutional complex is coming apart at the seams. Or better, the institutional gyves by which all previous peoples have been shackled are coming unwelded and are dropping off.

Does this mean that Western civilization is on the point of collapse? Are we witnessing *Das Untergang des Abendlandes?* Is eviction from the industrial Garden of Eden the penalty we must pay for eating the fruit of the tree of knowledge? From generation to generation there have always been some few who thought so. Something like this, I judge, is what Arnold Toynbee means by declaring that Western civilization is doomed unless it can find, or create, a new religion. On the part of many people, especially those less sophisticated than Toynbee or even Spengler, such "judgments" are in fact emotional reactions to the decay of some treasured institution or belief. But even after we have discounted institutionalized nostalgia, two serious difficulties remain for which the social scientists of the twentieth century are largely responsible. One is the failure to distinguish between two radically different kinds of social structures, and the other is the presumption that value judgments have no source but institutionalized mores. If "good" and "bad," "right" and "wrong," have only such meanings as they derive from prevailing social structures, and if there are no social structures save the ones that are now unmistakably falling apart, then we are in bad trouble. But is either of these suppositions correct?

Is social organization as such identical with what I have been calling "the institutional system"? Much of the literature of contemporary social science seems to assume this identity. In part we are the victims of our language. The *Shorter Oxford English Dictionary* defines "institution" as follows:

1. The action of instituting or establishing; foundation; ordainment; the fact of being instituted 1450. b. *spec.* the establishment or ordination of a sacrament of the Christian Church, *esp.* of the Eucharist, by Christ. Hence that part of the office of Baptism, and of the prayer of consecration in the Eucharist which consists in reciting the words used in institution (more fully *words, commemoration,* or *recital* of *i.*) 1538. 2. The giving of form or order to a thing; orderly arrangement; regulation. b. System; constitution 1821. [Italics of original.]

Such was the word in 1538 which we have been using since 1821 to refer to social systems!

We have also been misled by our failure to understand the technological process. In arguing that social structures—systems of interpersonal relationships—are not all alike I would begin with the technological process in its most elemental form. The use of tools—the performance of acts of skill—is itself inherently social and cooperative. Many tool operations—so many as to be characteristic of the technological process itself—require concerted, cooperative action by two or more persons, sometimes a great many more; and all skills, however individual, require to be learned. These are interpersonal relationships. They are dictated by the tools and materials themselves, and originate in no other way.

True, such organizational patterns are often "contaminated," as Veblen would say, by ceremonial considerations. But these quite unmistakably have another source altogether. They are not dictated

by technical necessity but express the supposed emotional needs—
the community-inspired compulsion neuroses—of the participants.
We frequently say—it is a cliché that echoes down the ages—that
the human way of life is possible only on the basis of superstition.
If so, what superstition? Or if any superstition will do, why not zero
superstition?

Clearly superstition is not a technological necessity. Is it nevertheless morally necessary? Is it true, as many writers say, that technology as such is neither good nor bad, that which it is depends entirely
on how it is used? Some even say this about knowledge, even, para-
doxically, their own knowledge.

Such presumptions are based on a belief which has prevailed
widely among contemporary scholars that values have none but an
emotional and parochial significance. This belief had its origin in
modern investigations of the phenomenon of belief. Those investigations of course revealed the institutionalization of belief: the rationalization of tribal mores in tribal legends, the emotional conditioning of all members of the tribe, and especially the children, to
the legends and their attendant mores, and the continuance of this
process throughout life by the regular performance of awesomely
moving ceremonies. Such investigations also revealed the univer-
sality of institutionalized beliefs and their attendant values, and
their parochial character everywhere.

By this discovery Europeans took a vast step forward from the
naiveté of their own local prejudice. But in denying the existence of
any other values than tribal mores, or any other process of valuation
than tribal conditioning, modern scholarship has been a bit hasty.
We are all creatures of emotion. But our emotions are aroused in
many different ways. Since strongly held value judgments involve
emotions (indeed, that is what we mean by "strongly held"), eminent scholars have declared that value judgments have none but
emotional significance. But surely this is an outrageous *post hoc*
fallacy! How the emotion was engendered surely makes a world of
difference! Institutionalized emotional conditioning does indeed produce emotional reactions. But does this mean that strong feelings
have no other source? If a scientist runs through the streets shouting
"Eureka!" does that mean that he is a victim of some barbaric cult?
Even the most intelligent people may feel strongly about issues
which they judge to be of the highest importance, perhaps just as

strongly as a savage feels about the infraction of a tribal taboo. But that does not establish that the judgment derived from the feeling, nor that the feeling was produced by tribal conditioning.

In addition to its confusion over the emotional content of value judgments modern scholarship has been confused about final causes. Every tribally institutionalized value system has its ultimate: what philosophers call its "final cause," by which presumably the entire train of value judgments is set going and toward the attainment of which every particular good is ultimately aimed. Modern scholarship has of course rejected the supposition that any such ultimate exists which is valid for all peoples, since no final cause has any meaning, let alone authority, in any community save the one in which it has its legendary being. It is this realization that has brought the doctrine of cultural relativism into being, a doctrine which now prevails widely among contemporary social scientists of all disciplines.

But by a curious twist of logic this doctrine, while establishing that no "final cause" exists except in the deluded apprehension of various tribal legends, nevertheless insists that value judgments can have no other source. But on what authority is this conclusion based? Obviously it is that of the mores—but no particular, emotionally validated mores—to which the scholars in question themselves might be supposed to adhere; just the theory of the mores. Thus in the very process of denying that tribal beliefs have any general validity, modern social science has dogmatically insisted on the validity of the tribal belief in "final causes."

Like the failure to differentiate institutions, this strange obsession with the doctrine of the "final cause" has resulted from the myopia which has prevented social scientists from seeing that value judgments of general validity are made every day—indeed, every hour of the day—by people of all parts of the world and of all the ages. The criterion in terms of which they are made is of course technological.

Considered instrumentally (as distinct from ceremonially) all human activities are causally related. As Dewey put it, every successful effort is the accomplishment of some end in view, and at the same time every accomplished end is a means to something else, whether it is a primeval savage swinging himself across a river on the severed butt of a trailing vine or a twentieth-century engineer stringing steel cables across "the narrows" at the mouth of New York harbor. To be sure, we can always ask, "Why cross at all?" This is a legitimate question, and the answer is significant. The myriad who cross all such barriers by all such means do so for a myriad reasons; but all these means and ends are related. However tangled and momentarily contradictory, all are woven into the web of the human life process; and all, taken together, constitute the answer to the question, "How has man reached his present estate?" This answer does not postulate unilinear evolution. Different societies have followed different routes, and some have led farther than others. No one questions that the cables of the Narrows Bridge swing farther than any vine. To be sure, any such crossing may be a mistake in terms of some particular tribal "final cause." It may violate some tribal taboo. But the fact remains that it is a step in the direction of further crossings, just as the Brooklyn Bridge was a step in the direction of the Narrows Bridge. If our ancestors were well advised to come down out of the trees, their descendants have likewise been well advised to improve their bridges. Neither judgment is, or can be, based on tribal taboo or "final cause." But all such judgments can be, are, and always have been, made in terms of process, finite but continuous. As Veblen said, more than half a century ago, "There is the economic life process still in great measure awaiting theoretical formulation." The challenge of institutional adjustment is that of continuing process.

In this paper I have not discussed any particular institutional adjustment which is now going on or which needs to be made. That, I assume, is the business of the other participants in this Conference. Instead I have tried to consider the underlying question which concerns us all, whether organizational adjustments are possible, or desirable, or necessary.

In doing so I have tried to make a clear distinction between the institutionalized and ceremonialized status systems which have prevailed so widely and so long in the history of mankind and the organizational patterns and devices to which mankind has been led by the effort to use tools effectively. Institutional traditions do not initiate changes. They are changed, principally by becoming obsolete. In the past this has come about very slowly, and primarily because technological development has changed the physical environment. But it now seems to me that a far more revolutionary change is in the making, one that affects the continued force of the institutionalizing process itself.

As I have tried to show, an essential element in this process—the one that binds together status systems, their mores, their legends, and their ceremonials—is the emotional conditioning of whole communities of people to the imaginary world of supernaturalism. Modern technology has changed the physical environment of mankind: even more important than that, however, may be the effects of modern knowledge, the power to know, which is the inseparable accompaniment of the power to do. This process—the demythologization of modern culture—is generally known. Not so generally understood are its inevitable consequences for the traditional institutionalizing process. That process, I am now convinced, has been short-circuited, and that is why all the traditional institutions of Western society are now coming apart.

Does this mean the end of Western civilization? Is a free society one that is in process of disintegration? There is no law of the universe which guarantees to us that such is not the case. But human ingenuity does persist, as it has persisted in the past even in the most rigidly institutionalized societies. Even in the midst of a welter of nonsensical taboos mankind has always discovered ways of cooperating in the use of essential tools. All the societies that have survived have done so, obviously, because in spite of their crippling fantasies they have been technologically viable. This power of intelligent cooperation still remains; indeed, it is more potent by far than ever before, as indeed it must be, since the tools we now manipulate in concert are more complicated and more potent than ever before. Furthermore, the challenge we now face is not that of invoking ancient superstitions and restoring irrational compulsions. Our task is to devise efficient organizational expedients and instrumentalities to do better—more fruitfully, more comfortably, more expansively—what the ancient devices have done, by which mankind just barely managed to stay alive from millennium to millennium.

Happily we do not have to start from scratch. In our adjustment theorem we "have-given" Western civilization as it is today, our extant society, absurd and contradictory in many respects, but still a going concern, indeed a growing concern. Our problem is only to insure that its growth is sound and healthy, not catastrophic and suicidal. Furthermore, the expedients we propose to use are never wholly untried. On the contrary, like those of all technicians, they are combinations and projections of existing organizational devices of well-tried efficiency which, used in new combinations, may prove vastly superior to their original components.

In short, the process in which we are engaged is one of pragmatic adjustment. We are already well embarked upon this course. Already ours is a largely pragmatic economy. Abram Bergson has recently used this phrase to characterize the latest developments in the Soviet economy, but it is too good a phrase to waste on Communists, especially since pragmatism is a distinctively American word. In fact, pragmatism is a uniquely American philosophy. It means something more than momentary resort to experimentation: it means the adoption of pragmatic adjustment as a way of life. What we propose is to invent organizational arts to match our science and technology, and by their use to grow into all the complicated arts of associated living.

KENNETH H. PARSONS

The Institutional Basis
of a Progressive Approach
to Economic Development

Economic development policies in the economically underdeveloped countries of the world must face the issue of the degree to which violent revolution is to be accepted as an instrument of economic development. It is clear from the history of this century alone that a violent revolution which destroys the existing order—political, economic, and social—entails sufficient social cost to give any patriotic leader cause for considering alternative ways of transforming the traditional structure of institutions and power.

We do not propose in this essay to argue the relative merits of development by revolutionary or peaceful means.[1] We accept the general view that major changes in institutions and the distribution of power are essential to development, and recognize that sometimes such changes may require revolutions of some sort. Accordingly our concern rather is to attempt a formulation of the central issues in a theory of institutional adjustment, which can serve as an integral part of development policy regardless of the rates of change in institutions. Some such conception is prerequisite to a progressive modernization of institutions.

We call this a quest for a progressive approach to institutional adjustment—in which "progressive" is intended to signify crucial

[1] This has been done recently by a number of readings in Laura Randall (ed.), *Economic Development: Evolution or Revolution?* Heath Studies in Economics (Boston: Heath, 1964).

elements in the process of institutional adaptation such as has been
achieved in the Anglo-American experience. This does not mean that
we shall argue that the Anglo-American pattern of institutions can be
superimposed constructively upon other countries and cultures. Instead, the thesis, or hypothesis, is that an understanding of the strategic practical necessities in this long history of relatively peaceful economic, political, and social development should, if elaborated in
theoretical form, have relevance to the decisions which must be made
in the development policies of the emerging nations. The processes of
constructive, or creative, institutional adjustment are almost un-
imaginably complex. But the experience of centuries of relatively
successful experience in institutional adaptation should yield significant clues regarding the issues inherent in the processes.

Within this general view of the problem, we shall first review
briefly a few of the key institutional transformations and innovations
in the history of the Anglo-American economic development and then
inquire whether the methods of institutional adjustment and the
beginnings of formal institutional development in the Anglo-American experience have relevance to the problems of institutional adjustment and innovation in the less well developed countries. Although
there have been many wars and revolutions in the Anglo-American
history over the past nine hundred years, still this continuum of experience is relatively stable, with economic development having been
achieved within a context of a gradual transformation of institutions.[2]

We should also note explicitly that both the policies for economic
development and the ingredient institutional adjustments require an
integral relationship between state and economy. These two entities
work together through the institutional structure of an economic
system.

In this brief comment, which must be selective, we shall draw
heavily upon the analysis by John R. Commons, especially in his
Legal Foundations of Capitalism; we shall also adopt his definition
of an institution, namely: The social practices or working rules by
which collective action restrains, liberates, and expands individual
action.[3] This conception is broad enough to embrace the customary

---

[2] The experience of some of the continental countries, especially of Scandinavia
and the Low Countries would probably serve as well, but their history is of somewhat less relevance to the U.S.

[3] John R. Commons, *Institutional Economics* (New York: Macmillan, 1934;
Madison: University of Wisconsin Press, 1959), p. 73.

practices, which simply grow unnoticed out of the experience of a people, as well as the deliberately instituted rules for the organization and guidance of economic activity—conventionally referred to in economic literature as the social framework of the economy. The conception also recognizes that institutions liberate as well as restrain.

As we interpret this conception of economic institutions, it has two functional dimensions which need to be clearly distinguished. One function is as a coordinate in the processes of production and distribution. Here institutions specify the general forms by which economic activity is organized. The achievement of economic performance— the producing, distributing, buying, and selling—is related to institutions as substance is related to procedure, or content to form.

Economic performance is stimulated, increased, or deflected by modification of the rules which guide and channel conduct. Arthur Lewis analyzes the role of institutions in economic development from this perspective. He terms it the consistency of institutions with economic growth, the latter requiring institutions which reward effort, assure recovery of investment.[4] This is the restraint, liberation, and expansion of individual action in Commons' phrase. Institutions are to be evaluated in this dimension by the ways in which they influence performance or productivity.

But institutions must also be understood in a second perspective: the social, historical, and time dimensions of the way institutions function in systems of social organizations. This aspect embraces the general relation of state and economy, and is referred to in gross terms as capitalism, communism, feudalism, and so on. These social, historical, and time dimensions of institutions present the more basic dimensions of institutional policy, for it is by their use that property is distinguished from sovereignty, and the great public purposes of order, security, freedom, and equality are made available to a people as value possibilities. It is this aspect of institutional adjustment to which this paper is directed.

The theoretical unity of a system of institutions, in this latter dimension, derives from the necessity for authoritative sanctions in the enforcement of working rules. This is the fundamental nexus of state and economy; the state enforces the key rules by which the economic system is organized and under which it operates. In pre-

[4] W. Arthur Lewis, *The Theory of Economic Growth* (Homewood, Illinois: Irwin, 1955), especially Chaps. II, "The Will to Economize," and III, "Economic Institutions."

state economies the customary rules are sanctioned by group or tribe, through a variety of penalties. In modern political-economic systems the general, strategic, or all-pervasive rules have the sanction of state, although many of the working rules are sanctioned by penalties imposed by private groups—such sanctions being permitted within the rules of state, without judicial notice being taken of them.

The original source of institutions, the raw material out of which institutions are shaped, is the experience of a people, struggling to survive through joint effort, seeking ways to settle disputes, attempting to make progress. The basic procedural issue in policy formation in the shaping of institutions is, therefore, that of how selections are made among experiences which serve as the source of the rudimentary practices that are elaborated and refined into institutions. A middle-way national policy for institutional adjustments would presumably both draw on the direct experience of a people as a source of rudimentary institutions, and adopt or borrow from the experience of other people as extensively as would be compatible with the integrity of the system of institutions of the borrowers. A complete xenophobia in such matters would certainly permit very little progress. At the opposite extreme, either a colonial policy which superimposes institutions or a wholly revolutionary approach to development assumes that the experience of a people and their institutional achievements are worthless, if not contemptible—worthy only to be destroyed. We are interested in exploring the middle way.

The Anglo-American Continuum of Institutions

Professor Commons once observed that "William the Conqueror was the founder of the Anglo-American economy."[5] The conquest of England brought a creative confrontation between the precedent customary society and the prerogatives of regal power. Although over the decades the powers of the crown approached the absolute, the Saxon people resisted and sought to recover powers and privileges taken from them by conquest. Out of these continuing struggles, the basis was laid for the creation of property rights—first in land.

William the Conqueror and his lawyers did not distinguish his property from his sovereignty. Both were possessions rather than property. He was

[5] John R. Commons, *Legal Foundations of Capitalism* (New York: Macmillan, 1924; Madison: University of Wisconsin Press, 1959), p. 324.

both landlord and king. The soil belonged to him by right of conquest, and the people were his subjects. Property and sovereignty were one, since both were but dominion over things and persons.[6]

The will of the king was supreme, and there descended from the crown that hierarchy of derived authority and the arrangements for reciprocal service called feudalism. We need to recognize that in an age of violence "the will of powerful individuals was the government" and that the primitive mind, which must have characterized most of the people, "could with difficulty comprehend anything but physical objects and individual persons."[7] Although by such phrases Professor Commons was characterizing eleventh-century England, similar human predicaments have been experienced throughout the world at such elementary levels of subsistence survival.

The general outlines of the glorious achievement of liberty on that isle are known to all, with Magna Charta (1215) a momentous event. The questions which interested Commons principally in his study of this epoch, and which are of interest to us, are those of how the liberty and opportunity were achieved, that were to become in turn the foundations of citizenship and property.

William the Conqueror and his immediate successors discovered, as have all dictators since then, that human beings have wills and interests of their own. These result, first and inevitably, in conflicts which must be resolved. As the representatives of the king travelled the countryside, assuming the judicial roles once exercised by the local customary courts, they found that an honoring of the customs of the people was the only efficacious way to settle disputes between landlords and tenants. From this root, under the systematizing concepts of judges, grew the common law.

But the ruler and his deputies also encountered the deeper psychological phenomenon, that people with wills of their own can only be induced, not commanded, to participate willingly and energetically in the economy: coercion is less productive.

During the six centuries that passed between the Norman invasion and the establishment of English colonies in America, the British people groped and fought their way toward the system of state and economy upon which the United States was built.

It was perhaps natural that the first major achievement of liberty

[6] *Ibid.*, p. 214.
[7] *Ibid.*, p. 215.

and opportunity came in agriculture. Land was both symbol and substance of wealth. The king was dependent upon his lords to provide soldiers for the realm, as well as food. Out of such necessities, there developed a series of confrontations between king and vassal: feudal dues of products, and services were converted to money rents; the royal privilege of holding land at the will of the king was gradually converted into an hereditary right of succession and occupancy, and eventually into the right to alienate land at will.

By the seventeenth century the process was virtually complete. The arbitrary powers of the crown, over the once subject people and things, were curbed by parliamentary procedures. The Act of Settlement of 1700 firmly established the basic principles which finally separated property from sovereignty, through a "compromise set of working rules" which Commons has characterized as establishing the devices of Collective Bargaining, Representation or Parliamentarism, Delegation of Power, and Official Responsibility.[8] The overall lesson for policy to be drawn from this experience is that the system of representative government, the principles of a free economy, and the independent judiciary, as well as the liberty and citizenship of a people, all evolved together. They form an interdependent whole.

In terms of land-tenure relationships, the great achievement of this era was the placing of limits upon the arbitrary powers of the crown regarding the use and occupancy of land. As a result, permanent occupancy and use rights were granted to the lords, previously tenants at the will of the crown. Dues and services were commuted to money rents, and came to be known as taxes: taxes were imposed only by Parliament. All these combined to dependably limit the arbitrary powers of the crown with reference to land.

As Professor Commons has analyzed this great transformation, the limits imposed upon the exercise of arbitrary power by the crown reduced absolute prerogative to a sovereignty exercised within the limits of constitutional restraints. This circumscribing of prerogative created an "indefinite residuum," leaving an orbit where the will of private persons was free.[9] This curtailment created both a field of opportunity for the use of land and zones of individual liberty for the former tenants.

[8] *Ibid.*, p. 104.
[9] *Ibid.*, pp. 220–221.

The working rules under which the (former) tenants could use the land evolved by the common-law method into the law of real property and even into the basic principles of constitutional law. The crown as sovereign retained rights in the land, which we now categorize as the powers to tax, the police power, and eminent domain; these in our tradition protect and implement the public interest in privately owned land. But beyond the scope of these reserved rights or powers, the successors to the former tenants became the de facto owners, enjoying the right to use and alienate the land by their own volition.

In terms of institutional adjustments, and particularly of the theory of institutions, this great episode shows the operation of several interrelated principles. (1) The exercise of the powers of the crown became stabilized so that a continuous authoritative exercise of the powers of government could be counted on. (2) Against this relatively stable exercise of power, it was possible to limit the exercise of royal power by gradually whittling away the powers of prerogative, reducing it to constitutionally exercised sovereignty. (3) These dependable restrictions on the zones of regal power created a residuum of opportunity and liberty, which, being protected as to prospective duties and exactions, was an open field for the exercise of the wills of the appropriate people—in regard to the use of land and the enjoyment of the achieved liberties. From these objective opportunities there has developed the structure of property; and from the protected liberties came citizenship, as persons became clothed in the powers of sovereignty. (4) The customary working rules of the relations between landlord and tenant were accepted by the state, through the judiciary, as the basis of the law of real property. The customary rules were made into property rules through selective adoption by the courts for use in the settlement of disputes and by the generalization into laws of the realm, under sanction of the sovereign powers of the state.

Political expansion and economic growth, stimulated by improved navigation, the discovery of the new world, the industrial revolution, and other advances, led to profound changes in the institutional structure of the British economy. During the sixteenth and seventeenth centuries the powers and functions of the guilds, as well as the monopolies based on royal grant, were curtailed. As Professor Commons observed, the guilds were chartered originally as units of "defensive capitalism." With economic growth these "defensive privileges" became "exclusive privileges."[10] To open up the occupations and to widen participation in commerce, the guilds were stripped of their previous public functions of settling disputes and making rules. Consequently those functions had to be assumed by the state, with the result that there developed a common law of business, parallel to the common law of the land.

Professor Commons has traced in some detail the wide array of institutional transformations that were achieved as an investment market-oriented economy developed in a parliamentary state out of the antecedent systems of feudalism, guilds, and state monopolies.[11] Two main points only will be noted: (a) The depersonalization of economic relations, and (b) The institutional adaptation to the time dimension of investment.

The primitive mind, Commons observed, could scarcely comprehend anything other than individuals and physical objects.[12] The domain of such attitudes had to shrink as a condition of wide participation in a market economy. The strategic point in this transformation was the depersonalization of contracts and promises to pay—the necessity, in Arthur Lewis' phrase, of dealing fairly with "strangers."[13] This depersonalization took the technical form of making negotiable both promises to pay and contracts for goods. Both were originally held to be deeply personal bonds between the two contracting parties, much as marriage vows are today. An efficient interdependent exchange system of commerce, credit, and investment was not possible until debts could be assigned without prejudice, and contracts became impersonal objects of business. "Modern capitalism begins with the assignment and negotiability of contracts."[14] From these roots has developed the whole structure of modern property relations—including the intangible property of equity stocks, and the incorporeal property of notes and bonds.

The investment necessary for the modernization of the market economy likewise forced the adoption of working rules designed to make the future reasonably secure. In a word, this requirement was

[10] *Ibid.*, p. 226.
[11] Particularly in the three chapters VI to VIII: "The Rent Bargain—Feudalism and Use-Value"; "The Price Bargain—Capitalism and Exchange-Value"; and "The Wage Bargain—Industrialism."
[12] Commons, *Legal Foundations*, p. 215.
[13] Lewis, *Theory of Economic Growth*, as at p. 45.
[14] Commons, *Legal Foundations*, p. 253.

met in the Anglo-American tradition through the development of a system of equity law, supplementing and complementing statute law and the court-made common law. Equity law creates uses and trusts, based on expected transactions, and also provides for preventative rules, whereby acts inimical to some interests can be forbidden—court injunctions are common instances. Whereas the common law provides for redress, for punishment after the offense is committed, equity law can forbid prospectively injurious acts. As Commons summarized it: "The remarkable expansion of the equity jurisdiction in the eighteenth century reflected the rise of capitalism based on pecuniary expectations, the corresponding subsidence of feudalism and the prerogative based on physical power. Thereafter it became possible for the courts to build up the law of business in proportion as business itself developed."[15]

If these few comments may serve to suggest something of the institutional transformation of the economy of England between the eleventh and the eighteenth centuries, we may now turn briefly to consideration of how these institutions took root in American soil, and their subsequent careers.

In the century and a half, approximately, during which the thirteen original states were colonies of England, the economies of the settlements remained very largely subsistence economies, supplemented by a substantial export crop economy in the southern regions. Economic development moved forward from this subsistence base. Efforts to establish a manorial system of farming were mostly failures. The early craftsmen did form guilds, and Professor Commons has analyzed the experience of the "Shoomakers" of Boston, which operated under a charter granted in 1648—evidently the only American guild which left a record of its activities.[16]

The critical event was, of course, the formation of the United States as a federal union, the combining of the separate states into one economic unit, under a constitution which made interstate commerce subject to national authority and gave markets a national dimension. Because of this extension of markets, the structure of markets changed very greatly, as is shown in detail in Commons' study of the shoe industry.

[15] *Ibid.*, p. 235.
[16] John R. Commons, "American Shoemakers, 1648–1895: A Sketch of Industrial Revolution," *Quarterly Journal of Economics*, XXIV (November 1909), 39–84.

These few references may remind us that the economic systems established on this continent were principally of the subsistence-handicraft sort with adaptations in agriculture to soil and climate. The systems were quite similar to those of Europe in the pre-market stage of economic development. The problem of institutional adjustment encountered by our forefathers with the achievement of independence has therefore some similarity to that confronting the new countries which have emerged out of the break-up of empires. However, the American situation was unique in some respects. The economy grew eventually to continental size; and the natives were pushed aside so that state and economy could both be started on "clean slates." But, as Commons observed, it is "this bald simplicity of American individualism, without much covering of races, armies, guilds, or prelates, that permits us to trace out all of the economic sutures in their evolution from infancy to manhood."[17]

Not only were the intellectual leaders of the colonies close students of English and continental thought, but they were also contemporaries of the great minds which shaped the liberal tradition of Europe. The early colonial leaders were contemporaries of Locke, Rousseau, Montesquieu, and Hobbes; and the drafters of the Constitution, of Adam Smith and Voltaire.

More than most systems of state and economy, the United States political economy was deliberately designed—its design being strongly influenced by the principles of classical liberalism. Into this design went wholesale transplantations from England. The British common law was accepted as the foundation of the legal system; the parliamentary system of representative government was adapted to both the federal union of states and the extended geographical scope of the system. The liberal principle of private ownership of land was basic to agriculture expansion and development. Also by the early nineteenth century manhood suffrage was widespread. This system was eventually capped by judicial review of legislation, as well as of lower court decisions, by the United States Supreme Court. The formation of limited liability corporations by permission of statute became a common practice by the mid-nineteenth century. With the legal sanctioning of labor unions and the outlawing of "yellow-dog" contracts in the 1930's, the institutional procedures were firmly established by which the system became an economy of group action.

[17] *Ibid.*, p. 78.

This whole system, merely alluded to here, can be characterized as one in which the "conditions of freedom" were firmly established in the formative period.[18] It was not a system in which the government was viewed as a merely negative or restraining influence. The public domain was distributed in ways intended to stimulate initiative; the powers of government were used as sanctions for private contracts, within the limit of the public interest. It was a system designed to release the energies of a people.[19]

In sum, the problem of institutional adjustment in America can be seen as two separate tasks. The first was the design and establishment of the system of state and economy as a going concern, through the selection of institutional procedures suited to this new situation; the second is the never-ending task of institutional adaptation to cope with the problems inherent in economic growth, the universalization of suffrage, technological progress, urbanization, expansion in population, and the growth of economic power in a market-finance-oriented economy.

As Professor Knight has observed, once the system was established, the practical problem changed.

The Wealth of Nations is the first "scientific" work on economics in that it gave a fairly clear and coherent picture of the nature and workings of a social economic organization on the pattern of free enterprise, with a reasonable minimum of political interference or control. In the course of time, England and the United States, and some other countries to a lesser degree, largely adopted this system of organization. Then the character of the practical problem changed. It became a question rather of examining the defects in the system and comparing the results with those to be obtained through some form of political control.[20]

The incremental institutional adjustments, once the system of state and economy was established, can be characterized with fair accuracy as a shift in the role of the state from that of a government sanctioning procedural rules for the organization of the economy, to a government participating directly in that economy. This increased state participation in the United States economy is achieved principally by regulatory and administrative commissions or agen-

[18] See Willard Hurst, *Law and the Conditions of Freedom in 19th Century United States* (Madison: University of Wisconsin Press, 1956).

[19] *Ibid.*, Chap. I, "The Release of Energy."

[20] F. H. Knight, "Economic Theory and Nationalism," in *Ethics of Competition* (New York and London: Harpers, 1935), p. 286 n.

cies, and is leading to the development of a new major field of law, administrative law, commensurate with the role of administrative commissions.[21] In the main, the state does not seek to own the means of production, but rather attempts to use the private purposes of investment, enterprise, and profit-seeking to serve the public interest through reconciliation of conflicts and the establishment of reasonable charges for services.

The Interstate Commerce Commission (1887) is a major landmark in the regulation of charges for private activities peculiarly affected by a public interest. Through his work on industrial commissions (initially to administer accident-compensation insurance programs),[22] Commons contributed significantly to the establishment of administrative commissions to mitigate the conflicts between capital and labor. One of his key ideas is that the interested parties—employer, employee, and the public—should all be represented and reach agreement on safety rules through investigation and compromise. The practices so recommended are promulgated as rulings which have the force and sanction of law.

From such simple starts as that for industrial safety through the industrial-commission device has grown the whole system of Social Security—humanizing the economy. Similarly, from the regulatory innovations instituted by the Interstate Commerce Commission has grown a large family of regulatory commissions, including those for agricultural adjustment which attempt to control agricultural output and prices, and the Federal Trade Commission, which attempts to keep economic power in check through limitations on the growth of monopolies and oligopolies.

With the assimilation of Keynesian economics into national policy through the Employment Act of 1946 and through fiscal and monetary policy, the functions of the state (Federal and State) in relation to the economy were rounded out not only to provide the original and basic public order (especially the rules for access to and participation in economic opportunities designed to release the energies of the people), the working rules of commerce, public services, and so on, but also to include among national policies measures for economic

---

[21] This characterization loses precision with extensive Federal expenditures for defense.

[22] Discussed in Commons, *Institutional Economics*, pp. 840–873; and *The Economics of Collective Action* (New York: Macmillan, 1950), pp. 277–284.

stabilization, the humanization of the economy, and the curbing of private economic power.

Professor Berle has aptly called this functioning whole the American Economic Republic.[23] The frontier of national economic and social policy is now the consideration of the plight of persons not included in this economic republic, through a complex of programs for education, civil rights, and development—called in 1965 programs to realize the Great Society. These current programs reflect an extension of the participating role of government in the economy to give attention not only to investment for the expansion of opportunities in particular areas, commensurate with the potentialities of the areas, but especially to the development of the capacities of persons now or prospectively lacking the abilities required for effective and rightful participation in a modern economic system.

The institutional adjustments which matter deeply in this economic republic face the eventual possibility of review and evaluation by the Supreme Court. The Constitutional provisions (in the 5th and 14th Amendments) that persons may not be deprived of life, liberty, or property without due process of law force the Supreme Court to adopt authoritative definitions of liberty and property. As Commons has shown in *Legal Foundations,* the original common-law conception of property, as physical objects held for exclusive personal use, has been expanded gradually to embrace the intangible anticipated value of expected market behavior, epitomized in stock shares in great corporations.[24] Seen in the large, these constitutional requirements for due process—with the correlative redefinitions of terms to accommodate changing economic, social, and political conditions—provide a great safety valve for orderly change. The working rules yield or give, before violence of revolutionary proportions can break out. This great device for institutional adjustment, an extension of the common-law method of rule making, might have manifold possibilities for the newly developing countries.

Institutional Adjustment in the Less Developed Countries

We have attempted a reconnaissance review of innovations and adjustment in economic institutions in our own tradition. The ques-

[23] A. A. Berle, *The American Economic Republic* (New York: Harcourt, Brace and World, 1963).

[24] Commons, *Legal Foundations,* especially Chap. II, "Property, Liberty and Value."

tion, then, is whether the Anglo-American experience holds meaningful possibilities for institutional adaptation in less developed countries.

During the past five or six centuries both economic development and the correlative adjustment in institutions in the less developed areas of the world have been swept along by the expansionism of a dynamic Europe. Although the systems of state and economy in most other areas were shaped less definitively by the liberal philosophy than in the United States, the liberal influence was widely and profoundly important. Private property in land, and the forms of parliamentary government were general phenomena. These institutional innovations met with only limited success over most of the world, with the result that much of the revolutionary ferment of this century has turned to the elimination of such establishments. One of the keys, therefore, to the estimation of the possibilities of the gradual approach to institutional adjustment, as we have experienced it, is through inquiry as to how the prerogative powers of government were transferred to, or superimposed upon the areas which came under the conquest of Europeans (including British), during the sixteenth to the twentieth centuries.

The twentieth century is quite unlike the preceding ones, in two major respects: (1) The number of independent nations has doubled, approximately, with the break-up of empires, giving to scores of new nations both the opportunity and the responsibility to create their own systems of modern institutions; (2) The European-centered, western conceptions of state and economy are now challenged by powerful states with a Marxian-derived political philosophy and theory of institutional adjustment. The European-centered monopoly of economic and political dynamism has ended. The Communist powers are now world powers, intent upon sharing their ideas and extending their influence, forcing upon the Western European nations a political and economic competition not experienced during the five hundred years preceding the Russian Revolution. This fact not only complicates the tasks of institutional adjustment, nation by nation, but also places upon us, as professional people, the need both (a) to understand the intrinsic difference between a Marxian-derived theory of institutional adjustment and one derived from western liberal principles, and (b) to consider ways in which a tolerable middle ground in institutional design can be achieved in a state, to mitigate the pressure from both the extreme left and extreme right. Unless professional people skilled in the design of institutions and cognizant of the institutional basis of freedom and opportunity accept this challenge, the task of institutional innovation will be abandoned to revolutionaries who understand neither freedom nor opportunity.

Since development in a nation-state must always take hold of situations as they are, we may usefully attempt to distinguish major classifications which place the problems of institutional adjustment in relief, region by region and even nation by nation. Two principles of classification appear to go far in sorting out situations in underdeveloped countries so as to identify major combinations of issues in economic development and institutional adjustment. One set is based upon a scale of development from a subsistence to an exchange economy; the other set which seems promising distinguishes the ways in which the powers of prerogative of the European governments were superimposed upon the conquered areas. Only in the western hemisphere, Australia, and New Zealand has the assumption of sovereign powers by new states been operative for a length of time sufficient for indigenous governments to take definitive form.

The contrast between Latin America and the other new countries in these three areas is striking. The U. S. system of state and economy (outside the slave South) established the rules of freedom which made opportunities and liberties objectively secure and meaningfully accessible through policies of widespread landholding, rights of voluntary association, and public education—all made operative within a system of representative government, universal franchise, and an independent judiciary. In Latin America by contrast, with such exceptions as Costa Rica, national independence replaced colonial administration by systems of centralized government in which virtually all powers of state, economy, and society were concentrated in the hands of a few families—who virtually owned the countries and the right to govern. The outcome, at the dawn of this century, was that a meaningful citizenship was enjoyed by only a few; the Indian population and those descended therefrom were characteristically excluded from the establishments.

Parallel to this political dualism, such modernization of agriculture as had occurred was heavily concentrated in export enclaves. The ownership of land similarly was divided between two separate systems: one based on the customary common-law right and occupancy through settlement and use; the other on a legalized system

of property rights—derived from European law and conquest and
having the sanction of the state—which was superimposed upon
and basically conflicting with the traditional customary system.

The great disparities of power, wealth, and status have in our
time led to social and economic tensions of paralyzing proportions.
The problems of institutional adjustment in this vast area are therefore complicated by the reform issue, which has already broken out
into revolutionary violence in a few countries.

Nevertheless, the liberal tradition has sufficiently deep roots in
Latin America that representative government seems to be a virtual
condition of long-run stability. Slow grinding processes are at work,
separating out the exercise of sovereign powers of government from
the privileges of public officials and the properties of private persons.
Along this line of adjustment, institutional change needs to be directed to providing an economic basis for a significant citizenship—
such as by an independent middle class. In agriculture this line of
adjustment means not only modernization, but also the establishment of a secure and independent tenure status for a substantial
proportion of the farmers.

In Asia and Africa the situations are more fluid than in Latin
America, excepting that population pressure limits the scope of adjustment in several countries (including Egypt).

In Asia, including the Middle East, the numerous military revolutions, from that of Kemal Ataturk down to the present, seem to
testify to a nearly absolute need both for a stable continuing exercise of the authority of the state and for the constructive participation of the state in economic development. Typically these military
revolutions have been directed against relatively ineffective parliamentary governments which were, or were claimed to be, controlled
by the influential few. The countries under military rule now seem
to be in situations which have significant similarities to feudal England. The distinctions between sovereignty and property, public
and private, and taxes and rent, are all currently blurred. Citizenship
in these countries—those retaining monarchs, as well as those ruled
by military groups—is at best a privilege. Policies for the private
ownership of farm land reflects, as in the earlier era of England,
an interest in enlisting the willing participation of the cultivators;
but such private ownership is supported more out of forbearance
in the use of the powers of prerogative than in the necessity to honor
either property or liberty according to due process of law.

National independence has come so recently to Africa that the countries are still in the stage of finding stable identities. A major factor here is the abrupt termination of government and the disintegration of public order, by withdrawal of the sanctions of external (colonial) prerogative. Until a self-imposed order is achieved, little development is possible. The critical initial institutional adjustment, therefore, is again in the way in which public authority is concentrated and exercised.

Cash crops have been added[25] to the traditional subsistence agricultural economies in a number of different ways, each with a distinctive institutional base. The simplest and the crudest method (and the one used by our ancestors in this country) was simply to push aside the natives and establish commercial agriculture by European settlements—the practices being rationalized by the rules of conquest, possibly facilitated by legalistic interpretations of the tenure rights of sheiks and chieftains. The indigenous people remained in the traditional subsistence economy, probably nearby, and sometimes worked as laborers on the modernized farms. With national independence, most of these European settlements in Africa are being liquidated—sometimes in an orderly way with the government in charge, sometimes by a sheer reversion to the antecedent subsistence system, with customary claims to land use and occupancy replacing the legally sanctioned property rights in land. A middle-way method is illustrated by the Gezira in the Sudan. Here a traditional agricultural system was replaced by a modern system— in which modernization included development by irrigation. The native peoples remain as cultivators, but as share croppers of the developing agency rather than as customary owners of lands. A third method is that of adding cash crop enterprises to a traditional subsistence agriculture—sometimes by expanding an indigenous or acclimated crop, such as palm oil; sometimes by adding a new crop such as cotton, coffee, or cocoa. In either event the traditional agriculture is modernized and to some degree transformed.

The nature of working rules concerning the rightful occupation of the land differs in these approaches to development. In the first the rules of the economy are derived from prerogative; in the third from customs. Professor Commons has observed that there were

[25] The exploitation of mineral and timber resources has followed a somewhat different course, but the principles of institutional adaptation seem to be similar to those in agriculture.

two original sources of the Anglo-American political economy: the exercise of the prerogative, of which statute law is the lineal descendant; and customs, the source of the common law.[26]

Our limited study of Africa leads us to think that there are unparalleled needs and opportunities for institutional adjustment by the selective modernization of customs through the common-law approach. An understanding of the nature and function of customs should make possible the achievement in a decade of deliberate policy and planning for institutional adjustment as much progress as was made in a century of slow adaptation in the Anglo-American tradition. The traditional systems of tenure in Africa have had as their implicit public purpose the security and survival of the group —family or tribe—rather than economic progress. The attempt by Europeans to create property rights in land through the exercise of prerogative has led to disorder, dissatisfaction, and social disintegration. Yet the modernization of agriculture requires that institutions should support and encourage investment in land improvements as well as stimulate the willing participation and the efforts of cultivators for development. The case for building upon customs, in the modernization of those institutions which are deeply intimate to life—such as land tenure and creditor-debtor relations—seems very strong. Although this has been recognized by some scholars (as evidenced by Dr. C. K. Meeks, in his *Land Law and Custom in the Colonies,* and others), development economists have given little consideration to these possibilities.

Finally it seems of major importance for the design of economic institutions to recognize that the people in the traditional societies of Asia, the Middle East, and Africa are not as individualistic as are westerners. Their systems have not been pulverized by individualizing revolutions such as occurred in Europe at the break-up of feudalism. Economic development in these areas therefore poses institutional problems different in many ways from those experienced in the United States. Such societies find socialism attractive. This is partly a dramatic way of rejecting a capitalism which they identify with colonialism. But the issues run deeper. Historically, in their situations, individualism would have meant starvation; and the prospects of individualism even now are chilling. Thus in agriculture, for example, the task of institutional adjustment for the next

[26] See Commons, *Legal Foundations,* p. 241.

few decades, at least, seems to require the design of a new mixed system with a balance between institutions which support individualism and modernizing institutions using group action. This latter seems to require a new kind of family or village farm-firm, be it an association, a corporation, or a cooperative. Within such a system, management, market, and credit orientation would presumably be the responsibility of the head man—with individual and family status within the concern determined by a set of "shop rules" rather than by property relations to commodity and credit markets.

We may take hope from the fact that the great historic achievement of the western world has been the realization of freedom and plenty out of a preceding despotism and poverty. These accomplishments did not just happen; they were achieved. The issue of achievement was faced squarely by the founding fathers of this country. As Hamilton remarked in the opening paragraph of the Federalist papers: "it seems to have been reserved for the people of this country, by their conduct and example, to decide the important question, whether societies of men are really capable of establishing good government from reflection and choice, or whether they are forever destined to depend for their political constitutions on accident and force."

WENDELL GORDON

Orthodox Economics and
Institutionalized Behavior

IN RECENT YEARS much of the effort of economists has been addressed toward the identification of constant relationships and equalities: examples include constant demand and supply elasticities, constant marginal propensities to consume and import, and equalities between saving and investment, spending and income, and demand and supply. If such relations can be identified, analysis can proceed and decisions on policy may be made accordingly.

The conception of these constant relationships and equalities fits into the institutional theory as examples of unchanged behavior patterns, behavior patterns which are unchanged during the period of time that an institution remains static. But it is exactly at the time of crisis, when the institutionalized and rigid behavior patterns are undergoing modification, that the most important decisions are to be made; and it is precisely at such times that the assumption that the elasticities and propensities are constants is most dubious. Let us look at some examples.

The Equalities

THE CLOSED CIRCUIT

First let us look at the so-called circular flow process that is now commonly used (especially in elementary economics textbooks in the United States) to summarize macroeconomic relations. This

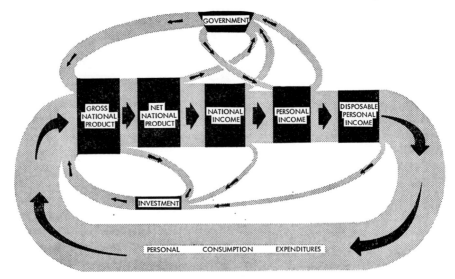

I. NATIONAL INCOME-FLOW DIAGRAM

particular diagram appeared in the third edition of Bach's *Economics.*[1]

The diagram seems to say that the return to the factors which create the gross national product is the purchasing power with which that same block of gross national product is taken off the market. If true this would be an important natural equality. But this is patently not necessarily true.

On the contrary the goods produced in a given year may be taken off the market with current year income, with the income of earlier years, or with money (as distinct from income) created either this year or in earlier years. Or the goods produced in a given year may be held as inventory, voluntarily or involuntarily.

SOURCE OF EXPENDITURE OF GROSS NATIONAL PRODUCT

The funds which take the gross national product off the market (or finance its retention as inventory) may be identified as follows:
$$E_{64} = (\ldots Y'_{62} + Y'_{63} + Y'_{64}) + (\ldots M'_{62} + M'_{63} + M'_{64}), \quad (1)$$

[1] George Leland Bach, *Economics* (Third ed., Englewood Cliffs, New Jersey: Prentice-Hall, 1960), p. 89. The approximate reproduction is used with the permission of the publisher.

Where:

E_{64} refers to expenditures in 1964; Y' refers to such of the income of the year identified by the subscript as is spent on GNP in 1964; and M' refers to such of the net change in the money supply as occurred in the year identified by the subscript as is spent on GNP in 1964.

A possible modification of this formula might be:

$$E_{64} = (\ldots aY_{62} + bY_{63} + cY_{64}) + (\ldots \alpha M_{62} + \beta M_{63} + \gamma M_{64}). \quad (2)$$

The symbols Y and M now refer to the total incomes of the earlier year and the coefficients (the a's, b's, and c's) indicate the proportion of those magnitudes that will be applied to expenditure in 1964. The coefficients are examples of constants which, if identifiable, would be of the type mentioned at the beginning of this paper.

DISPOSAL OF INCOME

Also an equation to represent the disposal of income might look somewhat as follows:

$$Y_{64} = (E'_{64} + E'_{65} + E'_{66} \ldots) + (M'_{64} + M'_{65} + M'_{66} \ldots) + S. \quad (3)$$

The money income of 1964 may be spent in any year from now to judgment day. Also the possibility exists that segments of the money of 1964 may be killed off as contractions in the money supply in later years. "S" is Saving. There is a kind of ambiguity about the relation between holding or destroying money and monetary saving. This model alleges that held money is saving and destroyed money is not. In monetary terms this distinction may be defensible, in real terms it is probably not. It is debatable whether symmetry requires a similar investment, or "I," term in equations (1) and (2).

KEYNES ON SAY'S LAW

In my innocence I assume that I am saying little more than Keynes said in the passage in the *General Theory* denouncing Say's Law of Markets (the well-known Law of Supply and Demand):[2]

. . . the conclusion that the *costs* of output are always covered in the aggregate by the sale-proceeds resulting from demand, has great plausibility, because it is difficult to distinguish it from another, similar-looking proposition which is indubitable; namely that the income derived in the

---

[2] John Maynard Keynes, *The General Theory of Employment, Interest and Money* (New York: Harcourt, Brace and Company, 1936), p. 20.

aggregate by all the elements in the community concerned in a productive activity necessarily has a value exactly equal to the *value* of the output.

This is a way of saying that the equality between spending and income is an automatic equality. It is not dependent on the proposition that a given block of income is expended on the purchase of the goods whose cost of production was involved in creating that block of income. A closed circuit is one thing the economic process is not.

Spending Equals Income (Downstream Flow)

What this means in terms of the flow diagram is that economic process is not appropriately described with a closed circuit flow diagram. All money spent is *ipso facto* received by somebody. There is an equality of sorts. But perhaps the equality is best represented by a cross section of a river which might look something like the accompanying diagram. One cross section is expenditure (= income) in 1961. The other is expenditure (= income) in 1962.

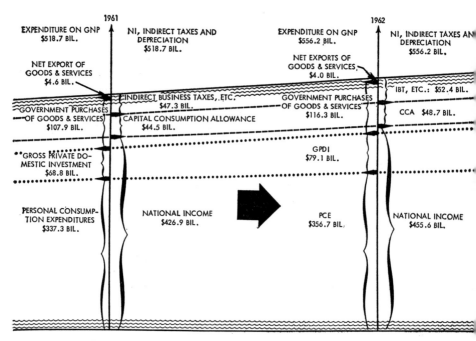

II. UNITED STATES EXPENDITURE AND INCOME

Perhaps it is needless to say that the river is flowing from left to right.

One side of each vertical line represents spending, the other side represents the receipt of spent funds. And the line gradually moves from left to right with the passage of time as the river flows toward the sea.

If everything is taken into account, the equality between expenditure and income is continuous and automatic. For the automatic equality to exist, there is no necessity that the income flow around a nonexistent circle and be spent on the goods for whose production the income represents payment. Instead the given income may be spent on goods produced last year, or some other year, or it may not be spent at all.

INVESTMENT EQUALS SAVINGS

Another automatic equality, which is much belabored in national income theory, is that between saving and investment. It is a bit difficult to find this equality in the national income accounts of most countries, including the United States. It is a bit hard to find, for example, in Figure II. But in Figure III effort is made to piece it together for the United States from United States and United Nations data.[3]

On one side of each vertical line is an estimate of monetary saving, on the other side an estimate of monetary investment. The equality is automatic. It corresponds in that respect with the precepts of both neoclassical and Keynesian economics. And it is almost entirely trivial in the sense that it tells us little about the nature of the forces that at one and the same time control the size of both saving and investment, the forces that determine the width of the river.

The identity itself is the result of defining as savings a group of items that add up to equality with the group of items classified as investment.

Inclusion or exclusion may be fairly arbitrary. In the frame of reference of the national income accounts of the United States, something called savings may be vented in a manner which has no other effect than bidding up the price of real estate. This is to

---

[3] *Survey of Current Business,* XLIV (July 1964), 7–40; United Nations, *Yearbook of National Accounts Statistics,* 1963 (New York: 1964), *passim.*

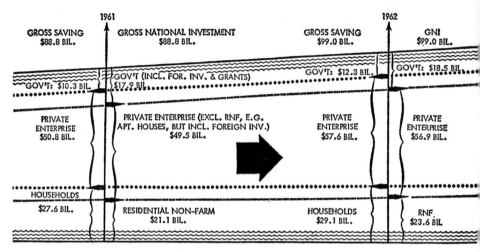

III. UNITED STATES INVESTMENT AND SAVINGS

say, if I interpret the national income accounts correctly, that an increase in the money value of real estate is handled as investment, or as an increase in the capital stock of the nation.[4] Nothing has been added, but investment has occurred.

We have been talking about monetary saving and monetary investment. The two are made to equal each other as a result of the definitions given to the concepts. Real saving must also equal real investment because of the nature of the definitions of those concepts which are generally given in economic theory.

But in real terms the saving which supports a given bit of real investment is the effort that goes into the creation of the capital equipment. And this is effort that might have been used to create consumer goods or might have been unexpended, never exerted. It is unnecessary that someone make a decision not to spend money in order for real saving and real investment to occur. In fact the equality between real saving and real investment means little more than that some effort and resources must be expended to create capital.

Assuming a given bit of real capital creation is to be financed with

[4] United States Department of Commerce, *National Income, 1954 Edition* (Washington: Government Printing Office, 1954), p. 60.

money, the money may even be created out of whole cloth.[5] Effort to specify the equality between money saving and real investment runs into all sorts of trouble. Of course the equality could be worked out with the help of all sorts of imputations assigning money values to things that are never sold for money and with appropriate allowances for the creation and destruction of funds. But the equality so established is a most fragile concept indeed, which has a very limited usefulness in the analysis of economic problems. The connection between real investment and voluntary monetary saving is indeed tenuous.

THE RELATION BETWEEN SAVING AND INVESTMENT IN REAL PROPERTY

Voluntary personal saving, or funds that might well become voluntary personal saving at the whim of the owner, may, as a result of institutional rigidities, be vented in other directions. This circumstance has relevance for the oft-heard statement that the predilection for land or property ownership in underdeveloped countries may absorb savings and frustrate capital formation. Traditional economic theory has seemed to say that this could not be.

But it is surely true that money in hand, which might be used to finance capital equipment accumulation, may be used to purchase land. Idle sources that might, *at that time,* be mobilized to create capital are, in fact, not mobilized. And this diversion of funds may be repeated over time by the subsequent holders of those funds. The institutionalized preference for land ownership may determine this behavior.

Of course if one does not define funds spent in bidding up the price of land as saving, no saving has been dissipated on land. But this is quibbling over semantics. And the real question is whether the institutions of a society at a given time are or are not willing to mobilize a certain amount of available and otherwise unused ef-

---

[5] The drawing out of the equivalent monetary saving (failure to spend) which is envisaged in period analysis, as such analysis is applied to national income theory, is a trivial logical exercise. The nature of the logic of the process is such that the savings are merely a residual drawn out regardless of the real content of the economic relations, regardless of the magnitudes of the propensities to consume and save, regardless of the length of the period-analysis period, and regardless of the stage in time when the process is cut off. Also the analysis blithely disregards the implications of the possibility that temporarily saved funds may be spent at a later date, or else calls this phenomenon the accelerator effect.

fort and resources to produce capital, or whether they are going to use the funds that might serve this purpose to buy land.

An institutionalized predilection for land ownership can in a very real sense divert energy from more constructive enterprises. And I believe that is what is meant by the statement that a predilection for land ownership in underdeveloped countries can absorb saving or, at all events, function as an alternative to the utilization of monetary saving in real investment.

INVENTORY ACCUMULATION

Another type of insight into the nature of the macroeconomic process may be obtained by looking at the role of inventory accumulation.

Perhaps a given unit of consumer goods is produced; and the factors of production are paid for producing it. But, for the nonce, the goods are unsold. They are inventory—perhaps, so far as the producer is concerned, thoroughly undesirable inventory. But so far as the necessary equalities are concerned, the income that has been generated is offset by something we shall rather arbitrarily call expenditure. It is investment in (and "expenditure" on) the inventory, made involuntarily by the businessman. Perhaps he got the money he used to pay the factors of production, other than himself, out of his sock, thus tapping earlier profit. Perhaps he borrowed it at a bank, which created it against fractional reserves.

Now if, at some happy day in the future, the businessman sells this undesirable inventory of consumer goods for a price higher than the sum he has paid out as income to the other factors, the increased amount is additional profit. The equality between expenditure and income still exists. Both expenditure and income at that future time are increased by the amount of the bonanza. Personal consumption expenditure is increased, as is corporate profit. And the river is wider.

Like the purchase of property, inventory accumulation is (and is not) capital formation. It absorbs savings, or does not, depending on how one chooses to define his terms. The production of unsalable inventory, even though alleged to involve saving and investment, produces nothing worth having as long as the goods are unsold.

CREATION OF USABLE FUNDS

Banks may create and destroy money. Their rights and duties

along this line represent one of the most important examples of institutionalized behavior in our society. Financial intermediaries
other than commercial banks may also create and destroy purchasing power.[6] One might go further than Gurley and Shaw and allege
that any individual or institution holding purchasing power should be
considered to have destroyed it until such time as he chooses to use it.
And at the time he chooses to use it, he creates purchasing power.
Actually the only thing keeping an individual from creating money
by writing IOU $100 on a sheet of paper is the lack of general
acceptability of the paper, lack of general acceptability which is
due to the fact that most people do not know him or his credit rating
and also due to the fact that people are institutionally conditioned
to expect money to be on engraved paper. Gurley and Shaw identify
several spots in the economic process where purchasing power may
be created or destroyed and claim that the creation and destruction
of purchasing power at some of those places may make a difference
in effect on real national income. It is not, they say, automatic that
the role of money is neutral in the economic process.

The argument may be extended to apply to the use and disuse
of purchasing power by people in general. And study of the foibles,
oddities, and rigidities of institutionalized behavior may give a better clue to the nature of the uses that are made and not made of
money and of effort than can a theory based on the assumption of
pure competition and of motivation based on effort to maximize
profit.

A bank (Latin American or otherwise) may create some funds
against fractional reserves and lend them, let us say, either to someone who will use them to finance inventory hoarding in an effort
to corner some market and make a speculative killing or to someone who will use them to produce goods, or even capital goods. In
one case development will be stimulated and in the other case not.
And the determining factor may well not be the rational laws of
pure competition but the mental sets which are a by-product of institutionalized behavior.

Constants (Propensities and Elasticities)

Up to this point effort has been made to describe economic process as a model in which certain things are necessarily and auto-

[6] John G. Gurley and Edward S. Shaw, *Money in a Theory of Finance,* (Washington: Brookings Institution, 1960).

matically equal and to identify in several cases the meaning of that equality. But more important questions are involved in the manner in which economics handles cause-and-effect relations. What is the nature of the forces that determine the magnitude of both elements in the equalities, the width of the river?

In economic analysis it is increasingly common to allege that these relations are controlled by constant behavior propensities and elasticities. These constants are fed into the so-called functional equations of economics and the effect of change in something such as investment on something such as income is then quantified.

In the Keynesian analysis it is generally assumed that a change in investment has an effect on income which can be estimated with the aid of a constant called the "multiplier," computed from another constant called the "marginal propensity to consume." Income is then a function of investment; and a constant controls the functional relationship. Also, in price theory, constant supply-and-demand elasticities play the same sort of role. In production theory, the assumption that the production function in a given industry is linear and homogeneous (and is the same all over the world) plays an even more restrictive role.

THE SPENDING OF INCOME

The process by which income is spent may be visualized in terms of the instantaneous multiplier of Keynes or in terms of period analysis. In terms of period analysis, during any given period of time the income of the period will be divided between spending and saving in the manner that the propensity to consume dictates. And the spending of that period becomes the income increase of the next period. For example see Table 1.

But this method of presentation may mislead as to the nature of the processes. For example, the failure to spend (saving) of a given period does not preclude the possibility that those, ostensibly saved, funds may be spent during some subsequent period, and they may be spent on either consumption goods or capital goods. Also the failure to spend (which is called saving in the period analysis) may literally have nothing to do with the formation of real capital. It is a residual of unspent funds apparently drawn out by a process that allegedly begins with an autonomous expenditure which may or may not in fact involve real investment.

An alternative way of looking at the period-analysis process may

TABLE 1

Effect of New Investment on Income, Consumption, and Saving

Assumptions: (1) New Investment of $1,000 (000,000)
(2) Marginal propensity to consume of ¾

	Investment	Resultant Increase in Income	Resultant Increase in Consumption	Resultant Increase in Saving
	1,000	1,000	750	250
		750	562.50	187.50
		562.50	421.88	140.62
		and so on	and so on	and so on
End Result Totals	1,000	4,000	3,000	1,000

help to indicate the nature of some of the inherent ambiguities. In-stead of a succession of periods of equal length, envisage a succession of initial periods of greater and greater length. Then the proportion of any given sum of income (or of change in income) which is spent may rise as the length of the period increases. The proportion which is saved may fall as the length of the periods increases. Immediately after the receipt of an increase in income none of it has been spent. All of it is, at least for the moment, saved. After a week, perhaps a quarter has been spent and three fourths is still saved (unspent). After ten years perhaps 99 per cent has been spent and 1 per cent saved. In the end some approximation of 100 per cent has been spent. Or the possibility exists that at any stage in the process the spendable funds may be killed off.

Then, to follow the further adventures of a segment of the spend-ing of any one of the periods, that segment becomes somebody's income and will initially be largely saved and in the end largely spent—or killed off somewhere along the way.

Such a line of thought suggests that in any given multiplier type problem the resultant effect on income, instead of being the tradi-tional three, four, or five times the amount of the autonomous in-vestment, is likely to be much larger, verging on infinity, or may approximate zero—depending on the length of a period. And there is a sense in which these are the answers which the multiplier model should give.

This different perspective on the nature of the process of period analysis does not refute the proposition that a quantity of saving (failure to spend) is drawn out by the process in an amount which corresponds with the amount of autonomous investment which started the process off. But it does indicate the essential triviality of that relation which means little more than that all the money put into circulation must be in somebody's possession at any given time, perhaps moribund, perhaps biding its time before being respent.

A major contribution of Keynesian theory was the indication that prior voluntary personal saving is not necessary to get the investment process going. But it was no service to imply that investment draws out *subsequently* an equivalent amount of meaningful saving. The real investment and real saving occur at precisely the same instant. And income is not necessarily related to investment by an identifiable constant.

The interpretation of the Keynesian instantaneous multiplier poses problems that are similar to and yet different from those posed by period analysis. For one thing, the instantaneous multiplier can tell nothing as to the process by which the described result is effected. At least the period analysis tries, even though in a misleading manner, to describe the process. The standard diagram for describing the role of the instantaneous multiplier is well known.

Figure IV describes a relation involving a constant propensity to consume and an effect on income which is dependent only on that propensity and on the amount of investment. And yet the manner in which investment is made may itself either influence the quantity of other investment or the spending pattern. The fact of investment in the production of an item such as the automobile (having tremendous consumer appeal) may affect spending habits, that is affect the propensity to spend itself. Or the knowledge that the government is building (if it were) adequate living facilities and providing adequate medicare for the elderly would probably encourage middle-aged people to spend a higher proportion of an increase in income.

Such qualifications to the Keynesian theoretical model have been generally recognized. But their implications for the theoretical usefulness of the model have not been generally taken into account, I believe, when time comes to apply the theory. There is doubt as to the appropriateness of attempts to compute constant marginal propensities and then to use them to try to predict the future. However, these reservations about the Keynesian model do not discredit the great usefulness of the proposition that spending increases income, whereas saving does not.

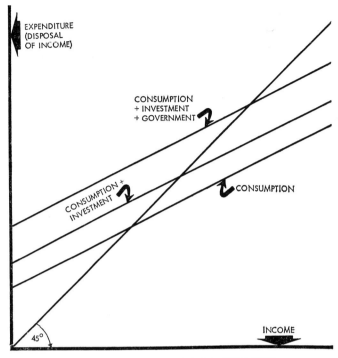

IV. NATIONAL INCOME THEORY

My complaint is not against an increase in spending (whether or not euphemistically called an increase in investment). I am all for increased spending. The complaint is against the proposition that we can predict the effect of the increased spending on income by the use of a constant multiplier. Depending upon the institutional setting of the particular increase in spending, its effects may go no further than the first use of the money. Saving may be 100 per cent in the first stage. A good deal of Reconstruction Finance Corporation lending in the early 1930's worked this way. Or, if the money is a subsidy to some people I know, it will all be spent. Then during subsequent periods, particular blocks of funds are killed off; other blocks are used in their entirety. The proposition that these tendencies average out to a constant multiplier is dubious.

CONSTANT PROPENSITIES AND ELASTICITIES

It may serve a useful purpose to cite some examples of models which are dependent on the assumption of constant elasticities and propensities, elasticities and propensities which, perversely, are likely to be changed by the occurrence of the event the effects of which are being analyzed. The Joan Robinson and S. S. Alexander formulas describing the effects of currency devaluation on the balance of trade of a country are cases in point.

The Robinson formula using constant elasticities runs as follows:[7]

$$\Delta B = k \left[Eq \frac{\epsilon_f(1 + \eta_h)}{\epsilon_f + \eta_h} - Ip \frac{\eta_t(1 - \epsilon_h)}{\eta_t + \epsilon_h} \right]. \quad (4)$$

I is the quantity of home country imports,
E is the quantity of home country exports,
p is the home price of imports,
q is the home price of exports,
ϵ_h is the elasticity of home demand for imports,
ϵ_f is the elasticity of foreign demand for home country exports,
η_h is the elasticity of home country supply of exports,
η_t is the elasticity of foreign supply of imports,
k is the fall in the rate of exchange stated as a percentage,
ΔB is the resultant change in the trade balance.

The Alexander formula adds to the picture the national income theory propensities to import and save, and depends upon an assumption that they are constants to obtain a determinate result. The Alexander formula[8] in a abbreviated form runs:

$$B_{(P,Y)} = \frac{B_p + \frac{MPM_f}{MPS_f} (\frac{k}{1-k}) B_h}{1 + \frac{MPM_h}{MPS_h} + \frac{MPM_f}{MPS_f}}. \quad (5)$$

B_p is the change in balance as occasioned by price effects only (result of Robinson formula).
B_h is the balance before devaluation (viewed from the point of view of the devaluing or home country).
MPM_f is the marginal propensity to import of the rest of world.
MPS_f is the marginal propensity to save of the rest of the world.

[7] Joan Robinson, "The Foreign Exchanges," in American Economic Association, *Readings in the Theory of International Trade* (Philadelphia: Blakiston, 1949), p. 91.
[8] S. S. Alexander, "Effects of Devaluation," *American Economic Review*, XLIX (March 1959), 22–42.

MPM$_h$ is the marginal propensity to import of the devaluing or home country.

MPS$_h$ is the marginal propensity to save of the devaluing or home country.

k is the per cent devaluation.

These formulae depend on the assumption that the elasticities and propensities are the same after devaluation as they were before. But common sense would seem to indicate that the fact of devaluation itself is going to change the behavior patterns of buyers and sellers. And such change invalidates the constancy assumption and means that the use of the formulae to describe the change in the balance of trade is dubious.

One does not for certain even know the direction of the changes. If the spectator assumes that the devaluation has solved the problem that occasioned loss of reserves, the elasticities and propensities will adjust in a manner calculated to bring exports and imports into workable balance. But if the fact of devaluation convinces the speculators that the currency is unsound and likely to be devalued again, their subsequent activities can make it unsound whether it would have been or not. And further devaluations become inevitable.

The important problem then in appraising the probable effect of a devaluation involves some guesses as to which way that fine institution, the foreign-exchange-speculator mentality, will jump in response to devaluation.

One is reminded of the manner in which the stock market following the assassination of President Kennedy first reacted by falling drastically. Then two or three days later, when it was allowed to reopen, it reacted with a violent rise.

There is a place for an economist's art in appraising which way an institution will jump when it is finally forced to mend its ways. And the estimating of constant elasticities and propensities probably has very little to do with this art. To spell out what I am saying: I am alleging that the constants econometricians spend so much time trying to identify are likely to be irrelevant at just the time important decisions must be made to deal with current crises.

The Role of Institutional Theory

Much that is important in economics is to be explained in terms of circumstances under which institutional resistance to change finally crumbles. There are two aspects to the analysis: (1) the timing of the crumbling, and (2) the identification of the direction in which various components of the crumbling structure will jump. Quantifying the jump would be desirable, but efforts along that line are secondary to the understanding of timing and direction.

Identification of the conditions controlling the timing of the collapse of institutional resistance might be described as the problem of threshold resistance.

THRESHOLD RESISTANCE

For long periods of time the people in primitive, agricultural, or backward societies may strongly resist moving to town or shifting into industry. Then some attitudes change and wild horses cannot now prevent the young people of deep East Texas from migrating to Dallas and Houston.

The United States Army (not to forget the Navy) passed through the South Sea islands between 1942 and 1945, and those island people will never be the same again, and neither will the soldiers. Or, to make the language a little more technical, the demand curves of both groups will never be the same again.

The sudden respectability obtained by Keynesian economics in business and political circles in the United States during the course of the last year or two (1964–1965) may represent a major institutional change, even though Walter Heller has abandoned the ship, and even though it is hard to guess the manner in which politicians and businessmen will distort the Keynesian tools they now respect.

A Russian wheat-crop failure throws off estimates of the demand for wheat in 1964, which were based on estimates of demand and supply elasticities done in the usual manner. Khrushchev puts Castro back to raising sugar, in spite of Castro's industrialization ambitions, and the price of sugar, after rising in a spectacular manner in the spring of 1964, plummets.

Being a tourist is considered respectable, even a help to economic development one day, an unpatriotic effort to sabotage the balance of payments the next. The same is true of foreign investment, of importing, and even of serving in the army overseas. Even the conception of a balance of payments deficit is, itself, one thing one moment and another the next.

What convinced United States big business that it could live with

President Johnson's policies and could not live with the same policies when endorsed by President Kennedy?

Then there is the obsession for steel industries among economic development planners in Latin America and other underdeveloped areas, an obsession which could as easily become one for aluminum or cattle ranching.

Once upon a time a male student at The University of Texas would not have dreamed of carrying an umbrella. Now the umbrella is a real status symbol. Time was when ladies generally smoked cigarettes rather than cigars. Now it is a traumatic experience to decide whether to offer a Tiparillo to a lady.

It is generally true in the life cycle of an institution that it does not change perceptibly during a period of many years in spite of minor pressures. But then one fine day a somewhat stronger pressure (perhaps not a much stronger pressure) collapses the house of cards and completely changes the nature of the behavior patterns of the institution. The Bastille falls, the Winter Palace is stormed, the Mongols breach the Great Wall, 1910 comes in Mexico. A whole economic and social order (or something less) collapses—an order that only the day before had been thought to be firmly entrenched, at least by the incumbent United States ambassador as he left for home on a well-timed vacation.

Analysis of institutional change has some analogy with "sensitivity testing" in statistics. "A test item will *respond* or *not respond* to a certain level of test stimulus (e.g., a shell will explode or not explode when subjected to a certain shock)."[9] It would be nice if a formula could be developed which would describe the amount of pressure it would take to break down the threshold resistance of a given economic institution.

How strong a push does it take (how much technological change and of what types does it take) to force an institution to change its ways? There may be an analogy with the contraction of disease. A person may live for many years as a carrier of germs of a certain type without being incapacitated by the disease in question. But one day a slightly increased concentration of the germs may bring him down with the ailment. Or some outside event may shift his germs from pas-

---

[9] Mary Gibbons Natrella, *Experimental Statistics* (Washington: Government Printing Office [for the National Bureau of Standards], 1963), pp. 10–11.

sive to active behavior to the detriment of somebody else in whose face he insists on breathing. The disease ceases being endemic in him and becomes epidemic in other people. The foot and mouth disease may be endemic among cattle herds that have built up resistance and become epidemic when fortuitous circumstances move the disease to a different setting.

An institution changes its ways drastically (or collapses) when technical change acquires sufficient force to compel the modification, in spite of institutional resistances which are the stronger the longer the institution has been set in its ways and the more isolated it has been from the forces of change. But toward the end the collapse may be substantially speeded or delayed by whether the patient happens to go out on a cold rainy night and get a chill.

Fate, and external forces, and human will can play an important role in influencing the timing of institutional change. It is not easy to quantify the resistance of institutional thresholds.

I doubt that much can be done along the line of forecasting the timing of the collapse of institutions. But maybe inability to read the future and to time catastrophe or triumph is not our greatest problem. Probably most of us would not care for what we saw if we could read the future. And most of us, if we had a choice, would really not like to know ahead of time when we are going to become ill, or when some girl is going to stand us up, or when we are going to die. Prediction is not the chief job of economics. The chief jobs are the occasioning of change when we want change to occur and the correction of undesirable situations. And much can be done along these line without the ability to predict.

Attempt to quantify threshold resistance is probably the wrong way to approach the problem. We can perhaps develop methods for jolting undesirable institutions with shocks of increasing force until the desired change occurs. But the matter is not simple. It is probably not desirable to overwhelm an institution with far more force than necessary. And yet starting with shocks that are too mild may help build up the resistance of the institution so that it later takes a much more disruptive shock than would have been otherwise necessary. The South was not hit hard enough in 1954 and it has built up its resistance. Eisenhower should have acted with more authority. His personal presence in Little Rock might have prevented the occurrence of many similar incidents which have followed.

Intransigence in resistance to change makes the ultimate change far more drastic than would have been the case if moderate change had been accepted by the institution with a good grace in the first place. As a result of the intransigence of southern segregationists during the last ten years, the changes in the South will be far more profound by 1975 than would have been the case if the original Supreme Court decision of 1954 had been accepted quietly and quickly.

The intransigence of the resistance to land and tax reform by the Latin American wealthy could be the influence that determines that there is far more change in ownership patterns in Latin America than might otherwise have been the case.

Institutional change such as will permit the effective use of new technology is not necessarily of the sort that destroys a whole social and economic order. In fact it would probably be desirable if techniques could be developed for weakening institutions by just enough to permit desired change. The chaos that goes with the destruction of whole social and economic orders is, surely, not desirable if it can be avoided.

Let us look at a few institutional change problems in this more modest, and perhaps more important, setting.

Generally in Latin America access to the financial credit that might permit the establishment of a manufacturing plant that would employ a hundred workers is denied to the artisan already running a productive enterprise giving work to three or four (chiefly members of the family). Bankers who have to pick and choose among the people to whom they might lend money react against such people. (They may not wear a jacket and a clean white shirt.) This is part of banking mores. The bankers pick and choose in a setting where the bank is generally not loaned up to its potential and where there are, in the society and available to be put to work, productive resources which either are unemployed or are not being used in the most efficient way. But the presence of worthwhile projects does not mean that the bankers will support them.

Few businessmen would now defend the morality of a 16 hour work day and a 112 hour work week. But business in general was afflicting such hours on its employees not so long ago. The great steel strike of 1919 was directed against such conditions.

Businesses fought the minimum-wage laws on the ground that such laws were contrary to the marginal productivity theory of wages, although they would have been hard put to it to prove they were actually paying their workers their marginal product if the proof shoe had been on the other foot. But businessmen have generally found it possible to live within minimum wages which they have earlier sworn would be unbearable. Much of what business does in terms of wage rates, commodity prices, profit rates, and interest rates is the result of customary attitudes and practices rather than a result of rational pursuit of maximum profits in a competitive market. It makes one wonder how price theory based on competitive assumptions established its hold. But of course, once price theory acquired its hold a lot of economists acquired a vested, that is to say institutionalized, interest in defending the relevance of the theory of competition to the real world.

It is perhaps legitimate to work out a theoretical model explaining how a competitive economic system would work, note that the results seem desirable, and advocate policies pointing in the direction of competition. This is the antitrust approach to the regulation of monopoly. It may also be reasonable to use a model assuming competition to indicate that even under competition certain policy tools cannot be counted on to work in the desired manner. In fact J. E. Meade uses general equilibrium competitive analysis to demonstrate that the mutual use of trade restrictions by all countries could not be counted on to move the international order to a welfare maximum. But it is another matter—and not a legitimate procedure—to assume that competition actually exists and to advocate public policies based on a theoretical model that depends on that assumption.

It is frequently said that profits need to be attractively high to encourage enterprise, investment, growth, and what not. But what is "attractively high": 6 per cent, 12, 24, or 36 per cent? Entrepreneurs have twenty-four hours a day like other people. Maybe they would go ahead and show enterprise regardless of how low the profit rate might be. Or maybe the rate merely needs to be higher than it was yesterday, regardless of how high or low it was yesterday. Or maybe the entrepreneurs will sit on their hands demanding a higher profit rate until they are convinced that the possibilities for that sort of blackmail have been exhausted—at which time they will quietly go about their business, accepting the profit rate they had earlier claimed was inadequate. Or they might give up entrepreneuring. One thing we should be clear about. It is not true that a situation involving relatively high profit rates in a country reliably tends to increase the number of entrepreneurs in that country relative to the number of entrepreneurs in other countries, and that that country develops fastest which has the largest number of entrepreneurs. It is not even true that manufacturing develops fastest in those countries that have the highest profit rates in manufacturing. If these things were true Latin America and the Arab world should have forged to the lead in development long ago. There may even be something to be said for the proposition that lower profit rates improve the quality of entrepreneuring. However, I should not like to state such a proposition as a proven general rule. In fact the acceptability of certain profit rates (or profit-rate anticipations) to entrepreneurs is one of the most institutionalized attitudes in economic behavior. The rational, economic man is not only non-existent—he is impossible in an institutionalized setting where a flair for the exploitation of the status quo is a part of good business.

DIRECTION OF CHANGE

Institutional resistances break down. What happens next? The manner in which we have tried to analyze economic problems in the past may lead us to seek answers of the wrong type and to be frustrated when such answers are not to be had.

There are not, and probably cannot be, sure rules for appraising which way elements will jump when an institution is jolted out of a mold. In the South there may or may not be long-run animosity between Whites and Negroes. It is largely up to the Whites and to White leadership to decide. A period of institutional change is a crucial period when leadership can make much difference in influencing the direction of change. But how is one to forecast what tack leadership may decide to follow in troubled times? This might be the way one interested in forecasting or prediction would look at the problem. But this is the wrong way to go about it. The problem is not how to forecast (not how an outsider can guess what someone else will do). The important problem is to develop judgment in deciding what to do in dealing with the new situation. What is the desirable direction, and what policies will lead in that direction?

At times of institutional collapse human will can play an overshadowing role in influencing the direction that the new pattern of behavior will take. In fact it is at such times that individual will can exert a significant influence on the course of history. During the period while a static institutional order continues to prevail, the individual, regardless of his ability, can have little effect on the course of history. But an energetic and aggressive individual can have profound influence during a period of institutional turmoil. In Russia in 1917 Lenin seized a country in institutional turmoil, and he and a small number of associates erected a new institutional order.

For reasons that are not clear the new order of revolutionary leaders in Cuba, Algeria, Indonesia, and Egypt does not seem to show this knack. Rather their chief effort seems to be directed toward foreign adventures rather than effective domestic effort. Or perhaps I am wrong. It is much too early to be dogmatic.

Over our inability to forecast the future we should not weep. Instead we should relish the chance to play a role in using judgment in an effort to shape what the nature of that future will be. And what we desire of our policy tools is, modestly, that we know which way they work, not precisely by how much. So, we come to the role of the policy pattern.

The Policy Pattern

The institutional attitude which is most dangerous in the modern world is the one accepting the concept that nationalistic solutions to problems are not only appropriate but positively meritorious. But it is not enough for the idealist to add the United States to the list of sinners in this regard by pointing out, among other examples, that the United States sabotaged the United Nations *ab initio* by endorsing the big power veto at San Francisco or behaved improperly during the Bay of Pigs episode. That is history. And the country with clean coattails is hardly to be found. What should be done? Yielding on controversial issues to the not-so-peace-loving nations of the Soviet bloc is a betrayal of human dignity. But support of underdeveloped-country despots from Farouk to René Barrientos has also been a betrayal of human dignity.

General acceptance by that institution, the nation state, of the concept that policy tools for dealing with problems must be checked for appropriateness in terms of the problems facing other nations is the all important institutional change that needs to occur in attitudes if the world economic order is to be viable.

Incidentally, the important information that economics needs to provide and is capable of providing in many cases is merely the direction of change that will follow as a result of other changes. Imports will probably rise as a result of a rise in national income. We do not necessarily need to know by how much.

There does need to be international agreement as to the identity of the problems worthy of concern and as to the manner in which the available policy tools will be used in dealing with the problems. The individual nation should not, and should not be allowed to, solve its own problems with policies that make the situation of other countries worse. Economists should be working on the identification of a policy pattern which would permit each country to solve its legitimate problems without creating major difficulties for other nations.

As an example of what is involved let me suggest a model that identifies certain goals and then identifies a set of policy tools which, if used under the agreed-on conditions, should work in the right directions.

The model follows:[10]

COORDINATION OF POLICIES

Problems and Goals	*Policy Tools*
I. Level of Living	
A. Short-run	
1. Internal	
a. Income distribution as among individuals	(a) Progressiveness of income tax and expenditure patterns
b. Internal depression (depression unemployment)	(a) Financial policy: (i) Fiscal policy—involving relation among total amount of tax, borrow, and spend, rather than progressiveness, (ii) Monetary policy—quantitative and qualitative credit control
2. International	
a. Balance of payments disequilibrium	(a) An international legal tender monetary unit (and price and wage adjustments), *or* (b) Freely fluctuating exchange rates (but not both), and (c) Constructive free trade
b. Terms of trade	(a) Subsidies to ameliorate price fluctuations

[10] The supporting argument is developed in my *International Trade: Goods, People, and Ideas* (New York: Knopf, 1958), pp. 623–631. The table, which is very similar to one developed in that book, is used with the permission of the publisher.

       (b) Measures in the area of eco-
           nomic growth

B. Economic Growth
  1. Increasing rate among   (a) (i) Foreign investments, (ii) In-
     underdeveloped countries   ternational grants, (iii) Techni-
                              cal assistance, and
                       (b) Financial policy: (i) Fiscal
                            policy—public works and pro-
                            duction subsidy, (ii) Monetary
                            policy—qualitative credit control
                            and an international currency
                       (c) Institutional adjustment

  2. Prevention of stagnation   (a) Largely a problem in institution-
     in developed countries   al adjustment *and*
                       (b) Educational opportunities
                            (including retraining aid)

  3. International income   (a) Growth on low side, not retar-
     distribution   dation on high side
                       (b) Freedom of movement of people

II. Security
                       (a) Policies that contributed to im-
                            proved level of living, and more
                            particularly
                       (b) Freedom of movement of
                            people, *and*
                       (c) (i) "Socialized" medicine, (ii) de-
                            cent provision for old age,
                            (iii) unemployment "measures,"
                            and
                       (d) No war

III. Freedom of Action
                       (a) Freedom of movement of
                            people, *and*
                       (b) Freedom of transmittal of tech-
                            nical knowledge, *and*
                       (c) The Bill of Rights

General Purpose Tools
(1) International price comparability
(2) A "do as you would be done by" attitude

Unused Tools

(1) Commercial policies (tariffs, quotas, licenses, embargoes [except for genuine health purposes], discrimination, export subsidies, dumping, and cartels)

(2) Wage cutting.

There is hardly time here to work through the logic of the model, and I regretfully abstain. However, I do allege that the model has possibilities for permitting the solution of a nation's legitimate problems without making matters worse for other countries.

One should have no illusion that this model represents final truth. But I do believe that it represents the manner of looking at problems that should be concerning economists and international statesmen. There has been all too little thinking in terms of policy patterns in the postwar period by either the leaders of the newly independent countries or the leaders of the developed countries. For example, in their balance of payments crisis in the fall of 1964, the British used a messy hodge-podge of tools without much regard for effects on other countries.

The important demand which the underdeveloped countries should make against the Great Powers is not that the Great Powers should give them favored treatment—the pitch of 1964's United Nations Conference on Trade and Development held at Geneva. Far more constructive would be the demand that each Great Power (and the other small powers as well) should conform its policies to a reasonable international policy pattern.

The world could stand a few declarations of interdependence in place of quite a few of the declarations of independence that have characterized the postwar period.

If pressed, I should be forced to admit that much of this paper has been based on bland assertion rather than on hard facts. But I should like to allege in defense that a policy recommendation, based on a theoretical model that assumes competition, is operating in an even more dubious never-never land.

GUNNAR MYRDAL

Adjustment of
Economic Institutions in
Contemporary America

The Trends of Changes Now Underway

Introductory Remarks

IN THIS BRIEF ESSAY, I discuss the problems of the changes going on in the American economy and the American society as if they could be dealt with in isolation. I am abstracting them from changes in international relations and thus from the interplay of the latter with changes of conditions and policies in the United States. I will have to speak in broad generalities, almost in terms of *obiter dicta*. Indeed, my ambition can only be to present a skeleton of thoughts.

I may be permitted to refer to my conviction that explicit—even if by logical necessity vague—value premises are needed, not only for the practical and political analysis of what ought to be accomplished by means of public policies, but also for the theoretical analysis of the facts and of the relationships among these facts; these value premises should not be chosen arbitrarily but should be relevant and significant to the society under study. The value premises assumed in the following discussion are the ideals of liberty, equality of opportunity, and social justice. In the present context they will not be further elaborated. Here I would like to point out that, although my terminology is different, I find myself fundamentally in agreement with Professor Ayres when he stresses that in social analysis value judgment must be awarded "validity."

In practical and political analysis, reasoning straight from facts and explicit value premises leads, of course, to the construction of a utopia. If the value premises are realistic in the above-defined sense, that particular utopia may, however, depict the direction of change in the society under study and will, in any case, reveal alternatives important practically for possible political action. Any realistic analysis should, however, take account of the elements of inertia and resistance to change.

In this connection, I may also be permitted to recall that a quarter of a century ago, when I was deeply engaged in a study of a complex social problem in the United States, I early arrived at the view—which I then also expressed and motivated—that social scientists and, more broadly speaking, public opinion in the United States were unduly fatalistic and, in particular, underestimated the possibility of bringing about social change by deliberate policy measures. This bias in the perception of social reality had, as I saw it, its background in many elements of the country's ideological history. The bias had been fortified by several traumatic experiences of policy miscarriage, the two most important of which were the failure of Reconstruction after the Civil War and the failure of Prohibition. Experiences of the contrary type—for instance, the United States' success, against violent opposition and much scepticism, in putting into operation a federal income tax fully as effective as those in the Protestant countries in northwestern Europe—were disregarded.

More specifically, my analysis of the social forces at work led me to the conclusion that the development of race relations in the United States would soon show an abrupt change: the status of the Negro people—which had, on the whole, remained unchanged for six decades after the great compromise at the end of the 1870's—would begin to improve substantially. I was rather alone in forecasting this change in the development of race relations and this fact, of course, opened my eyes to the more general fatalistic bias in the national culture and made it necessary for me to attempt to understand its historical causation. It also strengthened my conviction that working with explicit value premises is the only means of avoiding biases.

Today, the radical policy measures taken under the impact of the Negro rebellion—which itself has been generated by the improved status, in various respects, of the Negro people, on the one hand, and, on the other, the trend toward increased unemployment and its concentration on Negro workers—testify to a changed attitude in the United States in regard to the efficacy of deliberate actions aimed at changing institutions. I feel, however, that much unaccounted fatalistic bias still lingers in American social and economic thinking. This bias is often related to the complex of ideas which we include under the label "laissez faire" and which only gradually is losing its hold over policy deliberation in the United States.

Closely related to the fatalistic bias mentioned above is another general bias which I traced during that study; namely, the conception of social institutions as typically only obstacles to social change. In my opinion, however, the entire attitudinal structure, which I called the American Creed and which is anchored in the Constitution and a whole system of institutions, was instead a force for change. In the longer historical view, this basic attitudinal and institutional structure has been a main determinant of development in the United States and will continue to function in that capacity, helping to destroy other institutions of a conflicting character. It was in this sense that I characterized the Negro problem as a moral problem of the Whites who had, and continue to have, almost all of the power. The recent happenings, which have occurred as a result of the Negro rebellion, have confirmed my views in this respect.

Those reflections have, of course, significance far beyond race relations. Ideals have a social reality and significance for actual development when they are institutionally grounded; institutions—or some institutions—are forces for change and not for resistance to change. More generally, social study that appears particularly "objective" because it avoids mention of the fact that people plead to their consciences is, indeed, unrealistic. This has relevance to Professor Ayres' point that value judgments have validity and to my views about the necessity of applying explicit value premises in both theoretical and practical analysis.

Institutional change thus has largely the character of a moral catharsis. As valuations different from the institutionalized ideals draw part of their support from opportunistic, false beliefs about reality, the intellectual catharsis that follows improved knowledge stimulates and supports the moral catharsis.

When I observe from some distance the present trends of policy formation as well as of public opinion in the United States and place them in historical perspective, I feel that attitudes and institutions are now changing rapidly and radically—on the whole in the direction of reason and the institutionalized ideals I referred to. On this point I find myself in agreement with Professor Ayres who in the last part of his paper sees the coming of an "organizational revolution": a fundamental alteration in the process of institutional adjustment. We have arrived at this consensus by different roads. Professor Ayres is inclined to characterize this process as a "de-institutionalization," while I want to stress that the breaking up of some institutions is aided by the vitalization of other institutions.

By this I do not mean to imply that a large part of the institutional framework of the United States is not of the character to resist the changes we both see coming and that there is not much double-think in the adherence to the institutionalized ideals of the American Creed. Generally speaking, I believe, however—and I understand that Professor Ayres agrees with me—that with the moral and intellectual catharses we now witness, the stickiness of those other institutions is gradually being eliminated and "reforms"—and ever more radical "reforms"—made more feasible. From one point of view this movement can be characterized as a growing preparedness to accept wholeheartedly the ideals of the Welfare State.[1]

Institutional Adjustments Aimed at
Speeding Up Economic Growth

Since 1961 America's GNP has showed an annual growth in constant prices of 5 per cent, which is about double what it was during the eight years of relative economic stagnation in the Eisenhower era. The present constellation of economic relations does not indicate an early end of this boom.

Of importance in the present context is the fact that this change in

---

[1] Sweden, which is more advanced as a welfare state than the U.S., and about as rich, has in the decades during which I have been an observer—and sometimes a participant observer—demonstrated a remarkable and accelerating "rationalization" in regard to the acceptance of institutional changes. Political parties are becoming part of a "service state" where they often compete in urging reforms. The mill of public committees set up to induce change, the activity of the proliferating interest organizations and of political assemblies on various levels up to the national parliament are ever more rapidly grinding out changes of institutions almost without creating any public stir any longer. Institutional adjustment is taking on the character of almost seeming to be "automatic," not needing much of a fight. There is thus a rapid increase in "institutional flexibility" and a growing acceptance that institutions should be viewed from the point of view of their functional ability to serve commonly accepted goals. I have no doubt that a similar change has been underway in the U.S. for a considerable time, though it is still quite far behind the stage it has reached in Sweden. America has come a long distance from Sumner's "stateways cannot change folkways."

growth rate has been accomplished by deliberate economic policy measures and that this is being stressed. The ever more common acceptance of the view that government should take responsibility for keeping the nation's business steadily expanding is a new thing, at least in the unconditional and radical form it is now expounded by the President and the Administration. To quote from the President's Economic Report to Congress in the New Year of 1965:

Since 1960 a new factor has emerged to invigorate private efforts. The vital margin of difference has come from government policies which have sustained a steady but noninflationary growth of markets. I believe that 1964 will go down in our economic and political history as the "year of the tax cut."

The President can now safely come out against "preconceptions of an earlier day . . . that hamper rational action," while the late President Kennedy's criticism of the "myths" was received very coldly. Johnson can explain that "recessions are not necessary" and promise the continuation of vigorous policy intervention to prevent them from occurring.

The specific policy measures being used for this purpose are manifold. In more ways than one they imply a break with institutionalized taboos. One of these taboos has been the principle that the federal budget should be balanced. Though this principle has previously been violated, such violations never occurred except under the necessity of events or under a feeling of committing a sin. Taxes had, in any case, never been cut for the declared purpose of maintaining an advance of the economy already underway.

The rapid change of attitudes toward fiscal policies can be gauged when we remember that, at the time when the late President Kennedy was first proposing the tax cut, a Gallup poll showed a majority of Americans against it, if it would bring the federal budget into the red. The decision-making mechanism of the American Congress is rightly criticized for its many built-in elements of reactionary inertia; but when the chips are down it is more responsive to public opinion than any parliament I know. The fact that Congress was prepared to act on this issue a little more than a year later testifies that the American people had, in an astonishingly short time, become prepared to give up a cherished American doctrine founded upon mythological thinking which American economists had done too little to demolish. In this particular case the intellectual catharsis was very much due to support from a number of prominent business leaders.

Monetary policy has likewise been geared to serve expansion by creating and preserving an easy-credit market. For the first time, the interest rate for long-term loans was intentionally freed from the institutionally close relationship to short-term interest rates in order to avoid transmission of pressures from the international money market. In addition to fiscal and monetary policy, the government can point to a wide range of policy measures for expanding business activities, markets, and demand in many fields which in several respects represented institutional changes.

Even more important is the declared intention to meet any sign of recession by determined policy action of the same unorthodox type. In particular, the President has warned that an effort to balance the federal budget "too quickly" is "self-defeating" in an economy operating well below its potential. The President has asked Congress to reconsider its procedures for fixing tax rates in order to permit quick action in the fiscal field. If Congress should follow that advice, the United States would be better equipped institutionally than any Western European country to adjust rapidly the tax structure to the needs of balancing the economy by unbalancing the budget.

Gold in particular has acted as a catalyst of irrational ideas. The institutional tie to gold of currencies has been responsible for much unnecessary underutilization of labor and capital capacity. The exchange deficit and, in particular, the outflow of gold was one of the reasons for the contractionist policies that were responsible for the relative economic stagnation during the Eisenhower era. The Kennedy Government did not accept this conventional view but held that only a progressive economy would provide the gains in productivity that, with reasonable price stability, would improve the competitive position of the United States in world markets. The Kennedy Government was least of all prepared, solely on the basis of the deficit, to tolerate inhibition of policies for getting the United States out of its relative economic stagnation. Gradually, a number of policy measures were inaugurated in order to close the exchange gap; many of these implied institutional innovation.

As the United States has now regained confidence in its ability to maintain international liquidity, an attack is being waged against even the fears attached to losing gold. An important step was taken when the President proposed that Congress eliminate as arbitrary, unnecessary, and, indeed, harmful, the requirement that the Federal

Reserve Bank maintain gold holdings against deposit liabilities if such a requirement should result in a restriction of credit. This did not encounter the criticism in Congress, still less the anxiety among the public, that it would have met a few years ago, and it was quickly passed into law. This action implies that another irrational institution, and a preconception in American thinking and policy formation, is on the way to being extirpated.

As my only purpose in the present context is to point to institutional adjustments actually taking place, I am not entering upon the economic analysis of alternative ways to balance or unbalance the federal budget or of ways to alter the institutional tie between the dollar and gold. I should add, however, that the changes I have chosen for illustration are elements in a much wider complex of institutional adjustments aimed at maintaining an expanding economy.

The Need for Speeding Up Economic Growth

When the rapid population growth at a rate of around 1.7 per cent is taken into account, the growth rate of the GNP attained and expected for the near future cannot be considered particularly high. If calculated per head, which is the more rational way, the growth rate has only been a little more than 3 per cent. As the countries most similar to the United States have a population increase of only around 0.5 per cent, a comparison in terms of the rate of growth of the GNP should decrease the figure for the United States by a little more than 1 per cent.

Unemployment has been decreased only from about 6 per cent to below 5 per cent. As the growth rate of the labor force will now rise from 1.2 to 1.7 per cent—in total figures averaging about one and a half million a year instead of one million as in the last four years—a continuation of the last four years' growth rate of the GNP, which is what the President and his Economic Council foresaw, cannot be expected to reduce the unemployment rate; it will most likely again begin to rise. Unemployment among teenagers is around 15 per cent; this rate in particular is bound to increase.

Meanwhile it is increasingly realized that in addition to the registered unemployed, a large number of people have stopped counting themselves as participants in the labor market because they do not think they can get jobs. This "disguised unemployment" implies, among other things, that the ordinary unemployment rate is in a sense "elastic"; every approach to full employment will increase the labor force by drawing in "disguised unemployed" and thereby slow down the decrease in open unemployment.

In addition there are all the "underemployed" with abnormally inferior productivity and low incomes as wage earners or as self-employed as well as the "unemployables." They too represent an "elasticity" in the same meaning, as a lowering of unemployment will give many of them a chance to become regular members of the labor force and acquire the training needed for keeping a job and improving skills. Every success in the "war against poverty" (see below) will have the same effect.

Together these two categories of people who, like the registered unemployed, are in abnormal situations as breadwinners, amount probably to at least as many as the reported unemployed and probably many more.

Achieving a full-employment economy in the United States would assume raising the growth rate of the GNP considerably. This will gradually come to be more widely understood and urged in public debate. If and when the unemployment rate begins to rise again, this recognition will almost certainly be forthcoming. The increasing recognition of the several categories of "disguised unemployment" will strengthen the motivation for raising the growth rate of the GNP.

Although raising the rate of economic growth is theoretically an easy thing, it will need a further substantial change—in the same direction—of attitudes and institutions. The fact that the new policies have proved conspicuously successful so far—and have not led the nation to bankruptcy—has pragmatic importance and will make the Administration, the Congress, and the general public prepared to take more of the same medicine, when once the issue of speeding up economic growth is brought up with more vigor.

The Problem of Balancing the Economy as Employment Increases

Although the present boom has left the various relations within the economy in "balance" up to now, it cannot be assumed that this "balance" will continue under all conditions, especially if economic growth is speeded up as considerably as I assume to be rationally motivated by the facts and the value premises.

In particular, the cost-price structure has not moved in an inflationary direction up till now; it is plausible that this is largely due to the huge fringe of open and various forms of disguised unemployment around production. Decreasing unemployment could then be expected to cause a push from the cost side.

This danger is considerably less because of the labor supply "elasticity" I pointed out in the previous section. Nevertheless, there are risks that in the market for very highly skilled labor or where very strong trade unions operate, wages could increase so much faster than productivity that an inflationary development would be the result. Similar risks exist in the markets for goods and products, particularly when the prices are "managed."

An acceleration of economic growth, therefore, increases the need for more economic planning on the national level and, in particular, for more intervention in the market than that represented by the price-wage "guideposts" set by the Administration. This will require the acceptance of a changed institutional structure for the relations between Government and the economy. As a matter of fact, there has been a gradual move in this direction.

This issue of how to speed up economic growth so as to approach full employment while retaining a balanced economy is still rather dormant in American economic policy debate. It is improbable, however that it will remain so.

Actually, the growth of the GNP during the last months has proceeded at a faster rate than forecast. Meanwhile, the Administration is continually proposing new stimulants for business and is actually now being pushed by business to take stronger measures, for example, by a larger decrease of the federal excise taxes. The shift to a situation where the United States will have to accept either a certain inflation of the wage and price structure or more government planning and intervention in the setting of wages and prices—or a combination of the two changes—may thus come gradually. As a matter of fact, this move has already been underway for some time.

Government planning and intervention have traditionally been resented by American business for not entirely rational reasons. In this connection I will restrict myself to stressing one general point. Government intervention should not imply more bureaucracy and detailed controls. What is generally needed is a more deliberate and better preplanned control of certain broad national parameters for the economic development. As a matter of fact, the United States, compared with most other rich countries such as Sweden, has an overgrowth of bureaucratic intervention, necessitated by the lack of rationally planned controls of those parameters.

The Need for a Speeded Up Change in the Structure of the Economy

The one regularity in the dynamics of human attitudes and behavior patterns that is almost a "law," as the term is used in the natural sciences, is Engel's law that as an individual's or a society's income rises a continuously lower *relative* share of that income is used to buy food. That law reigns, however, over a much wider range of demands. There is a limit also to the relative increase of the demand for manufactured products of all sorts, for transport, and for a number of services provided by private business—for instance, those of banks or of hairdressers.

These limits to demands in various directions, including those for food, have considerable flexibility. The quality of goods and services can be improved and entirely new ones offered, and demands can be stimulated. Indeed, more and more fancy goods and services can be pressed upon the market by more and more effective advertising. But the limits do exist. Their reality is, in the first instance, based on the fact that there are *other* demands which at higher levels of income and living claim a bigger share of the incomes—and should be doing it even more rapidly if people's real needs were rationally considered.

These other needs have some broad common characteristics. They are predominantly needs for *services* and not so much for material goods. Moreover, and this is the point I wish to stress here, they are to a large extent needs for *public* facilities of a nature that will make our communities more nearly perfect instruments for living and working and for education, health, personal care, and for culture in its broadest sense, including all the creative activities in science and the arts, and increasing participation in, and enjoyment of, these activities by wider strata of the population. Another increasing demand is for more leisure; but leisure will be more valuable when those other needs are better met. *Indirectly,* the provision of these services raises the need for huge investments that will mainly have to be *public investments.*

Within its proper realm, private business cannot possibly supply us with the facilities to meet these communal needs which should be rising as society gets richer; this is particularly true in regard to the needs of those who are not very well off (see below). This implies that we will have to change our economic and political institutions so that collective needs are recognized and satisfied by collectively organized supplies. The public sector should increase and increase very much and very rapidly. It is increasing but not nearly fast enough.

The impediments to such a change are very great, particularly in the United States. For one thing, the universal fact is that while people are quick to complain about the paucity and low quality of public facilities, they dislike paying taxes.

A second type of impediment to increasing the public sector is the deeply entrenched distrust of government, particularly of the central government. This is associated with the heterogeneity of American society and also its historical pattern of development by federation and the adherence to the political structure of new and remote territories. Along with this goes the traditional belief that government is inefficient *per se*. This belief has a basis in the fact that the United States for various reasons has been slow in developing an independent and competent civil service.

A third type of impediment has its origin in the huge effort that goes into advertising the products and services of private businesses —stimulating interest in and awareness of the possibility of consuming increasing quantities of goods and services which, according to the broadened Engel's laws, should be responsible for a relatively, though not absolutely, shrinking part of total supply. The publicity for what the community does to meet our needs is much less intensive; it is, indeed, often negative as this public activity is held on a quantitatively and qualitatively low level.

A fourth type of impediment to the growth of the public sector is the fact that the facilities its offers do not appear in the market, where an individual can immediately meet his slightest impulse of demand. I cannot go out and buy hospitals or schools for society as I can buy a house to live in and an automobile to take me around. To obtain new or increased public facilities assumes a lengthy and complicated political process in which most of the time the individual is not moved by an active and present need and is not pressured by commercial publicity; even thereafter there is usually the necessity of a time-consuming process of planning and plan fulfillment. Action tends to be "too little and too late."

The fifth and most formidable inhibition is, of course, that it is not only one's own but also other people's needs that are to be satisfied in the public sector. Of particular importance is the element of income redistribution which an increase of the public sector implies. It is the poorer strata that are most in need of being better served by the community. If, as in the United States, they are not well organized to press their demands, this inhibition becomes politically stronger.

The "War against Poverty"

The United States has become accustomed to having in its midst enclaves of very poor people, usually spatially segregated and badly integrated into society. In the last two to three years, there has been a rising tide of awareness in majority America of the need to lift these groups out of their poverty. The poor themselves had been astonishingly quiet—I have characterized this "underclass" as the world's least revolutionary proletariat—until the Negro rebellion which, however, up till now has not inspired other submerged groups to press more effectively for their interests. Without going into an explanation of these elements of the social situation in the United States in this context, I will restrict myself to pointing out some of the general relations between the "war against poverty" and other issues touched upon above.

The policies to eradicate the causes of pathological poverty in the United States will, to a large extent, have to consist of increased and improved public facilities for meeting collective needs, such as housing, and educational and health facilities. Pursuance of these policies will therefore help to promote the changes needed in the structure of the American economy in regard to a greater public sector.

In addition to that type of aid to the poor in kind, redistributional reforms will have to be pushed in regard to the Social Security structures, taxation, agricultural policies, and minimum-wage legislation.

Both types of policies will increase total demand, which is needed for speeding up and sustaining a more rapid economic growth. Their general tendency, and this is another particularly significant point, will be to change the direction of the expansionary economic policies from tax cuts to increased expenditures. At a certain point higher taxes will be needed, although the federal budget would still be expansionary and, perhaps, for certain periods unbalanced.

As already mentioned, insofar as these policies are successful in increasing effective labor supply and raising its quality to fit the labor demand better, they will make speedier economic growth more easily attainable without causing inflationary pressure.

Speedier economic progress will also facilitate increased public expenditures for eradicating poverty without corresponding tax increases. Insofar as speedier economic growth will reduce unemployment and underemployment, it will even more directly decrease the number of the poverty-stricken or will alleviate their relative poverty. At the same time it will render all specific antipoverty programs (for instance, retraining of workers and in fact all "uplift" programs in the health, educational, and cultural fields) more effective. As the economy approaches full employment, expenditures for these purposes will stand out more clearly as profitable "investments."

Even assuming a speeded up economic progress, one should not assume that advances in "the war against poverty" will be easy, cheap, and rapidly won. Thus far the specific reforms being carried out as an "unconditional war against poverty" are of relatively minor scope and some of the activity is spurious. The moral and intellectual catharsis is continuing, however. There is a flood of statistical investigations, conferences, books, articles, and political declarations testifying to this and at the same time keeping up its momentum. If economic growth is maintained and gradually speeded up, the majority of Americans above the poverty line will increasingly come to see the effects of poverty amidst plenty as a drag on economic progress. Pragmatically they will come to learn that even the redistributional reforms are productive and do not endanger, but enhance, their own income and profit prospects.

A Few General Observations

Operationally, many of the things proposed and attempted in "the war against poverty" must be carried out on the local level. This will raise to major importance the institutional problem of how to make local government in the United States more effective.

In this context, it seems probable that we will see more of central controls. In particular, it is incredible that the Federal Government, as it increasingly is going to assume responsibility for a large part of what had earlier been local financial burdens, will not come to press for uniform minimum standards, for instance in regard to school buildings and teaching, and for larger and functionally more efficient local government units. We have already seen the beginning of this type of induced institutional change, for instance in relation to federal aid for road building. Increasingly, segregation of Negroes will be counteracted.

The Negro rebellion will continue until all sorts of discrimination, even that of a merely *de facto* type not supported by laws and regulations, has been radically eliminated. American society is firmly committed to equality of opportunity, and there will not be social peace before this ideal has been realized. The trend will go in the direction of the ideal. As its fuller realization is not within sight, this means that relations on the racial front will be in flux for the foreseeable future.

One effect of all the things which will happen within the framework of the "war against poverty" should be a livelier participation of the poor strata in political life and, particularly, in elections. The Negro rebellion and the resulting federal law protecting the Negroes' right to register and vote has promoted that result more directly for this group. The Negro rebellion itself, as well as whatever is attempted and accomplished in the "war against poverty," should progressively spur political participation of other groups of low-income Americans as well. Broadly, this trend should in its turn support all the various changes of policies that have here been stressed as needed in the United States.

One remarkable aspect of what has happened in the United States in recent years, that in this context can merely be hinted at, is the change of business opinion in the direction of more "progressive" views. Outside business—and some professions—there is in the United States a great weakness in the institutional infrastructure, related to the low degree of "political" (in the wider sense) participation of people in the lower-income strata. In particular, the trade-union system is weak numerically and afflicted with serious shortcomings. In the interest of a balanced social and economic development, there would seem to be a need for radical reforms of the American trade-union movement, raising its ideological sights and preparing for its growth in size and unity and for intensified member participation. Whether, to what degree, and by what speed all the other changes underway will initiate such a trend in the institutional infrastructure in the United States, is an important problem worthy of intensive study and discussion.

FOREST G. HILL

The Government and
Institutional Adjustment

The American Experience

THE INSTITUTIONAL FRAMEWORK of the American economy obviously has undergone fundamental changes during the past two hundred years. This institutional change has been shaped and often initiated by governmental action. Indeed, there has been enough purposeful guidance of institutional adjustment to warrant further inquiry into the American experience with governmental planning of institutional change. Past efforts to plan or guide institutional adjustment have been episodic but recurrent; they have involved consensus and controversy, new thrusts and stalemates, compromises and reversals. However, the prevalence and scope of these efforts, extending from the Revolution to the present day, render them of far more than mere historical interest.

In the early 1930's the New Deal opened an era of great institutional change in which government has had a larger part than ever before. This era now seems to be far short of any real culmination, even a temporary one. In any event, we must face some basic questions concerning the character of the institutional adjustments and governmental functions which have actually evolved, which may be expected, and—most importantly—which should be sought. Comparative study of the recent experience of other countries will aid the analysis of these questions as they affect the United States. However, study of earlier American experience is equally essential; and it may have some significance for other nations, especially the younger and less advanced ones. Although this is not the place to ponder the relevance of historical "parallels" or the problems of finding "lessons" in past experience, it provides an opportunity to review our national experience in the light of current issues. This brief survey, while perhaps yielding some historical perspective, can do little more than outline what a fuller inquiry would require.

Several related questions should be considered in reviewing the part played by government in institutional change. How flexible or adaptable have American institutions been? To what extent has the adjustment of institutions been aided by government? To what degree has this governmental action been consciously planned? Along what strategic lines has the government exerted its influence, and in terms of what chief goals or purposes? Has this public action occurred at all levels—local, state, and federal? How has it been shared among the legislative, executive, and judicial branches? To what extent has such government action been conjoined with that of private groups? What have been the major impediments to effective action in reshaping institutions? On what grounds of ideology or interest—constitutional or sectional, economic or political—has public planning been resisted? What has been the historical pattern of ebb and flow of institutional adjustments? Although these questions can be little more than posed here, they provide both a perspective for this survey and a measure of the study yet needed.

Little need be said here about the colonial period with its liberal infusion of British institutions, values, and legal concepts. Although the mercantilist policies constituting the colonial system were determined in Britain, the American Colonies were allowed considerable leeway and self-government. Since there was no central British administration in the colonies, the individual colony remained the unit of government action. Each colony engaged in extensive regulation and promotion of economic activity, involving a great deal of home-made mercantilism as well as latitude for individual initiative. Deep-rooted precedents thus evolved for reliance on private enterprise and on government regulation at the state level. Although the colonial institutions of landholding had a distinctly feudal or manorial character, small-scale farming and land ownership in fee simple appeared in New England and began to spread.

To put matters briefly, the American Revolution accomplished a highly selective revamping of the institutional pattern. Such waning feudal institutions as primogeniture and entail were eliminated, and fee-simple landholding became the prevailing norm. The colonial period had left a heritage of animosity toward government-fostered land concentration and business monopoly and toward distant or centralized government. The individual states became the prime foci of government, and a relatively weak central government was created under the Articles of Confederation. The main accomplishment of this government had to do with planning for the public domain. The states having conflicting claims to western lands were induced to cede their claims to the central government, which proceeded to make long-range plans for settling and governing the public domain. These plans were incorporated in the famous land ordinances of 1785 and 1787, which provided for the survey of public land, its sale to settlers, and eventual admission into statehood. An unprecedented scheme for national expansion and self-government was thus created.

Immediately after the Revolution several urgent problems emerged which required a stronger central government, as many people soon recognized. Pressing need was seen for a uniform and adequate currency, nationwide protection of property and contract, control over western settlement, fulfilling of obligations to war veterans, unobstructed interstate trade, and a national military establishment. Difficult commercial and territorial issues with Great Britain were still unsettled. The situation was made more urgent by postwar deflation, disruption of foreign-trade patterns, disputes among states concerning trade and navigation, unregulated settlement in the West, unrest among veterans and debt-ridden farmers, and ominous demands for free land, debt relief, and paper money. The Constitutional Convention of 1787 recognized the necessity for some reordering of economic and political institutions. National defense, commercial stability, orderly settlement, and legal protection of property and trade were prominent among the interwoven long-range needs which this institutional planning had to serve.

The Constitution was, as regards both purpose and content, an economic as well as a political document. It provided a general framework for evolving political and economic institutions and for meeting major problems which had emerged or been foreseen. Economic determinism need not be invoked in order to emphasize the economic import of the Constitution or its formative effect on institutions. The federal structure, including the concept of limited powers and the scheme of checks and balances, reflected the heterogeneity of economic and sectional interests and recognized the clear precedents for state action and individual enterprise. The separation of legislative, executive, and judicial functions was central to this government scheme, especially as regards the protection of property and contract by the federal courts.

The general powers delegated to the federal government included powers to tax, borrow, and appropriate funds; responsibility for military, postal, and treaty-making functions; and control over foreign and interstate commerce. Trade with the Indians, then an important military and diplomatic question, was included. Other delegated powers of an economic character included coinage, patents, copyrights, standards of weights and measures, and bankruptcy. Concern about creditors' property rights caused the death of business firms, but not their birth, to be made a federal matter. The Constitution dealt with money in terms of coinage and mints; it did not mention banks, despite the fact that a few banks which issued bank notes existed by the 1780's. Along with most matters of trade and production, banking was presumably left to the control of state governments. Nevertheless, the constitutional powers of the new federal government were fairly broad in the context of the problems and precedents of that era. As is currently emphasized, the Constitution provided for the creation of a common market of potentially tremendous size, to be administered under uniform rules.

Early national legislation essentially fulfilled the Constitution's major provisions having an economic aspect. This legislation set forth the "rules of the game" for the national economy, structuring and complementing the functions performed by the state governments. Congress soon adopted a tariff measure and acted to monopolize the coastal trade for American vessels. Early laws made specific provision for coinage, weights and measures, the postal service, and like matters. The planful character of this legislation was demonstrated by the policies advocated by Alexander Hamilton as the first Secretary of the Treasury. Hamilton essentially assumed the role of a national economic planner. He advocated and worked to achieve a stronger central government, a liberal interpretation of the Constitution, and a comprehensive set of developmental plans. His program was largely contained in a series of reports he submitted to Congress. The major reports dealt with funding and assumption of the public debt, excise taxes, chartering of a national bank, coinage, and government encouragement of manufacturing. Hamilton's proposals regarding all but the last were enacted, resulting in a regularized national debt to be redeemed at par, a system of taxes and currency, and creation of the Bank of the United States.

Hamilton regarded these governmental functions as being highly interrelated and possessing great developmental value. The public debt, for instance, would augment the money supply and encourage saving and the desire to hold money claims, as well as assuring fiscal integrity and a sound credit rating for the new government. The Bank of the United States was a semipublic or "mixed" enterprise, with one-fifth of its capital provided by the federal government. Its functions included government loans, fiscal service to the government, note issue, loans to business and industry, dealings in bullion and foreign exchange, and central-bank relationships to private banking. Hamilton deemed it to be so essential an institution that the doctrine of implied powers justified the government in chartering it. His "Report on the Subject of Manufactures" (1791) advanced the classic infant-industry argument for the protective tariff. In this report he advocated other sweeping measures to promote manufacturing. These included encouragement of immigration, employment of women and children in industry, restrictions on the export of raw materials, bounties for manufacturers and inventors, public construction of roads and canals, and government inspection of manufactured products to improve their quality.

Hamilton was clearly willing to regulate as well as protect and subsidize in order to promote industrial growth. He rates as a pro-business interventionist as well as development planner. His proposals to foster manufacturing, however, did not soon gain favor. From 1789 to 1816 the tariff was primarily for revenue purposes. Tariff duties remained the chief source of federal revenue until the early twentieth century. Prior to the Civil War the second major revenue source was the sale of public land. As favored by Hamilton with his overriding desire to raise public revenue and encourage industry, early land policy called for the cash sale of public land in somewhat large lots at fairly high prices, thereby slowing the rate of settlement. This policy more often favored land speculators than small farmers; but it may have eased somewhat the scarcity of labor, as was intended.

The Hamiltonians and Jeffersonians held divergent views concerning the goals of economic development and the appropriate role of government. The Hamiltonians favored concerted and even forceful measures to foster a more diversified industrial economy, while the

Jeffersonians preferred agricultural expansion, free trade, and more state than federal action. On the crucial policy issues of that period the followers of Hamilton advocated high protective tariffs, a land policy to serve revenue purposes rather than rapid settlement, continuation of the Bank of the United States, and a liberal interpretation of the Constitution. However, the Jeffersonians favored low tariffs, cheap land, and strict construction. Their belief that the Bank of the United States was both unconstitutional and unwise caused it not to be rechartered in 1811. The Jeffersonians soon began to have their way about land policy and the encouragement of western settlement. Land policy was liberalized in 1800 and 1804. In 1820 the minimum lot size was again reduced and the price per acre was lowered. By 1832 a small settler could purchase as little as forty acres of public land for fifty dollars.

With regard to federal promotion of science and transportation the Jeffersonians were not always exceeded by the Hamiltonians. Jefferson wanted the Constitution to be amended to grant the federal government explicit power to execute river improvements, construct roads and canals, and create a national university. Indeed, every President prior to Andrew Jackson advocated the founding of a national university. Jefferson's objection to these federal activities evidently rested more on constitutional than on substantive grounds. As Secretary of State and then President, he supported the Patent Office, research on weights and measures, and plans for the Coast Survey. Constitutional scruples did not prevent his making the Louisiana Purchase in 1803, and he quickly dispatched the Lewis and Clark expedition to explore and determine the resources of this vast territory. As in all later western expeditions, scientists were included in this exploring party.

Jefferson established the U.S. Military Academy at West Point, New York, as a predominantly engineering and scientific school. He also supported the founding of two national armories which, together with liberal government contracts and advances of funds, nourished the creation of a small-arms industry in this country and helped Eli Whitney introduce the principle of interchangeable parts in the manufacture of small arms. During Jefferson's administration the construction of the Cumberland Road was commenced as a national project; its westward extension was continued under federal auspices until 1840. His Secretary of the Treasury, Albert Gallatin, made the famous "Report on Roads and Canals" in 1808. Gallatin stressed the joint military, economic, and postal value of his proposed network of improvements. In his plan the large, essential, unprofitable projects were to be constructed or financed by the federal government, while other links would be completed by state or mixed or private enterprise.[1]

Trading difficulties and reduced tariff revenues caused by the Napoleonic Wars and the War of 1812 prevented, or at least postponed, the execution of Gallatin's ambitious "national plan of internal improvements." Wartime difficulties, however, stimulated domestic manufacturing and acutely demonstrated the industrial and transportation needs of this country. The War of 1812 revealed the nation's vulnerability to coastal attack or naval blockade and its critical need for coastal fortifications, for technical skills in artillery and engineering, and for the capacity to send troops and supplies to points of unexpected attack. Along with this realization of national deficiencies, the war produced a great spirit of national solidarity and purpose. This "era of good feelings" produced sweeping plans for the joint purposes of defense and development. In 1816 the first protective tariff was enacted to safeguard war-born manufacturing against peacetime foreign competition. Tariff rates were raised progressively in the period up to 1833, when a compromise act scheduled a ten-year reduction. The second Bank of the United States was created in 1816 with the same functions as its predecessor but with greater size and scope.

As a young nationalist in the Jeffersonian tradition, John C. Calhoun of South Carolina initially supported tariff protection, the second B.U.S., and federal financing of internal improvements. Much later as a sectional leader of the South, Calhoun bitterly opposed all these policies. However, he served ably as Secretary of War from 1817 to 1825, made an imposing "Report on Roads and Canals" in 1819 updating Gallatin's comprehensive plan, and actively directed the War Department's execution of mushrooming defense and development projects. As early as 1815 this country began sending army officers to Europe, especially France, for study and the accumulation of military and industrial knowledge. The War Department recruited some of Napoleon's military engineers from a defeated France and used them as teachers of military and civil engineering at the en-

---

[1] See Carter Goodrich, "National Planning of Internal Improvements," *Political Science Quarterly* LXIII (March 1948), pp. 16–44.

larged Military Academy and as planners of a system of coastal
defenses.

For the latter purpose the War Department in 1816 created the
Board of Engineers for Fortifications. Its chief figure was a noted
French engineer, General Simon Bernard. This board made surveys
and project plans not only for harbor defenses but also for internal
improvements deemed to have military significance, regardless of
whether they were private or state or federal undertakings. The
board reasoned that adequate coastal defense had many interrelated
aspects: fortifications, the state militia, the army and navy, coastal
canals, road and river connections with the interior, harbor improvement, greater population and trade at the port cities, and general
industrial development. The board's reflections and plans appeared
in its "Report of the Board of Engineers on the Defence of the Sea-
board" (1821). The board then devoted increasing attention to the
interior of the country and to improvement projects of a more obviously civil and economic character. At this time the work of the
Coast Survey was expanding and the civil functions of the army
engineers began to increase rapidly. In 1824 the first regular river-
and-harbor bill was enacted.

In that same year Congress passed the General Survey Act, author-
izing the army engineers to make surveys and plans for roads and
canals which might be appropriate for federal execution or financial
support. To administer this act, the Board of Engineers for Fortifications was commissioned in the dual capacity of a Board of Engineers
for Internal Improvements. This planning board functioned until
1831, directing many internal improvement surveys and making numerous reports which were submitted to Congress. The Survey Act
remained in effect until 1838, serving as the vehicle for providing the
project planning ordered by Congress or requested by individual
states on behalf of their public or private enterprises. The trend was
from comprehensive to piecemeal planning, along with generous
engineering aid. Although the state of New York constructed its
Erie Canal between 1817 and 1825 employing civilian engineers, the
many other state and local projects which were prompted by New
York's highly successful venture typically took advantage of this
federal engineering aid.

Practically all of the early railroad projects, commencing in 1827,
used military engineers for the location, survey, project plans, and
estimates of their routes. While a few railroad projects were state

enterprises and others received state subsidies or loans, the great majority of them were private undertakings. President Jackson, who normally objected to most federal transportation projects other than the improvement of a few major rivers and harbors, seemingly did not oppose the supplying of engineering services to promising state or private transportation ventures. During the 1820's and 1830's, when transportation had a very high developmental priority and when civil engineers were few and poorly trained, the General Survey Act permitted the wholesale provision of government engineering aid. At the same time many army engineers, who had been trained at West Point and on government surveying teams, were leaving the service to become state engineers, chief engineers of railroad and canal companies, plant managers, and engineering professors in the new technical schools.[2]

The sectional deadlock which prevailed from the 1830's to the Civil War prevented the enactment of major new federal legislation. A perilous balance of free and slave states was maintained, and in the Congress a sectional veto confronted any large change in policy. This legislative stalemate held sway in such crucial policy areas as tariffs, disposal of public lands, regulation of banking, and federal aid to transportation. The trend of tariff rates was generally downward from 1833 to the Civil War, thanks to the South's bitter objection to protectionism. Although the South successfully opposed free land on the homestead principle, some stimulus to settlement was provided in other ways. The Pre-Emption Act of 1841 permitted settlers to take up land prior to regular government sale. Poorer land which had been passed over was reduced in price. In addition, veterans were given generous land rights. Liberal land and immigration policies jointly promoted western settlement, even without free homesteads. Between 1845 and 1853 the country reached its continental limits with the annexation of Texas and the Oregon country, the Mexican cession following the War with Mexico, and the Gadsden Purchase.

An attempt in 1832 to recharter the second Bank of the United States produced great controversy and a veto by President Jackson. Four years later its charter expired, leaving the banking field to the proliferating state-chartered banks, which were free of federal control. Many of these banks had opposed the Bank of the United States

[2] For an analysis of the developmental work of the army engineers during this period, see Forest G. Hill, *Roads, Rails and Waterways: The Army Engineers and Early Transportation* (Norman: University of Oklahoma Press, 1957).

for the twin reasons that its central-bank operations limited their note issue and lending activities while its branches competed for the available banking business. State regulation was reasonably strict in New England, New York, Louisiana, and other settled trading areas but was more liberal or indifferent in the agricultural states. In that period the various states adopted the principle of free banking, chartering banks under prescribed general standards.

There was a related movement toward general incorporation acts permitting other firms to incorporate if they met minimum legal standards. Prior to this time bankers and businessmen had been forced to seek special acts of incorporation from their state legislatures. This earlier scheme had become objectionable because of the established privilege, political favoritism, and monopoly abuses which it engendered. It had developed in a period of active state control over economic life when the corporation was regarded as a quasi-public agency or an instrument of state policy. Only special undertakings deemed to be of great public interest had been incorporated, with their charters often containing regulatory and monopolistic features. As business opportunity and the spirit of enterprise increased, the corporate device came to be regarded as an instrument of private rather than state purpose. The corporation was then privatized or democratized by state laws providing for free banking and general incorporation.

Although many states continued to construct or finance transportation improvements in the decades just prior to the Civil War, federal aid to transportation encountered great opposition and several reversals. Federal engineering aid to state and private enterprises was greatly curtailed by 1840. However, the army engineers made surveys for transportation projects on the frontier and in newly settled regions. They also built military or territorial roads and conducted many scientific explorations in the Far West. Their most notable work of the latter type was the survey during the 1850's of several possible railroad routes from the Mississippi to the Pacific. This surveying produced extensive data on the topography and resources of the Far West. Although there was much sentiment for federal construction of a transcontinental railroad, sectional fears and jealousies prevented agreement on a route. The army engineers continued to make river and harbor improvements, but this work fluctuated in volume and was occasionally suspended. The fluctuations were caused by sectional or local rivalries and constitutional arguments about a plethora of small local projects, while the suspensions resulted from periodically recurring treasury deficits.[3]

The federal government increasingly promoted ocean transportation and the advancement of science during this period. The navy was enlarged and the Naval Academy and Naval Observatory were founded. Naval personnel made oceanographic surveys, exploring expeditions, and maps and charts, all of which had both commercial and naval value. In 1845 shipping subsidies made their appearance in the form of mail contracts. Increased attention was given to the construction of lighthouses, the charting of the coasts, and the general safety of navigation. Government promotion of science for useful purposes thus became more and more varied. The army engineers included geological and mineralogical exploration in their work in the West. Various government personnel, including military surgeons and people from the Land Office and the Indian Office, collected weather data and other knowledge about the West. The Smithsonian Institution became a government research agency with strong interests in natural science. The Census Office expanded its activities, and the Patent Office by the 1840's was conducting agricultural research. Although constitutional and sectional issues often restricted federal execution and support of transportation projects on the eve of the Civil War, federal support of useful science was becoming quite extensive. Many of the leading scientific figures of the day were government scientists.[4]

Among its chief effects, the Civil War occasioned a legislative revolution. The decade of the 1860's is thus very prominent as a period of institutional adjustment. Major policy measures long stalemated by sectional conflict were rushed through Congress, once the southern states had seceded. Tariff rates quickly became highly protective and remained so into the twentieth century. In 1862 the Homestead Act was passed, providing free land for settlers, while the Morrill Act helped the states establish land-grant colleges for the educational and technical benefit of agriculture and industry. A federal Department of Agriculture was created to augment the scientific and statistical work previously instituted by the Patent

[3] Promotion of transportation at all levels of government is described in Carter Goodrich, *Government Promotion of American Canals and Railroads, 1800–1890* (New York: Columbia University Press, 1960).

[4] The relation of government to science prior to the Civil War is surveyed in my paper, "Formative Relations of American Enterprise, Government and Science," *Political Science Quarterly* LXXV (September 1960), pp. 400–419.

Office. Decision was reached on the route for a transcontinental railroad, with liberal government land grants and loans provided to the companies executing this project, which was completed in 1869. Land grants were made to several other railroads in the West up to 1871, when the practice ceased. The existing federal programs for transportation and science were bolstered by large appropriations. These included river and harbor improvement, the construction of lighthouses and western roads, and geological and mineralogical surveying in the West. During the war the National Academy of Sciences was chartered as an official scientific advisory agency, thanks in large part to the efforts of the government scientists.

Other legislative innovations produced by the Civil War had to do with financial institutions, slavery, and reconstruction. The greenbacks became the first paper money issued directly by the federal government. The federal income tax made its first appearance in American history—as a strictly wartime fiscal measure. The creation of the National Banking System irrevocably involved the federal government in the banking field. This system, together with the Independent Treasury scheme instituted by the federal government in 1846, constituted the main framework for this country's financial development until the Federal Reserve System was established in 1914. The National Banking Acts provided for the federal chartering of banks, allowed them to issue uniform national bank notes, and regulated their capital structures and cash reserves. These acts, along with a prohibitory tax on the note issue of state-chartered banks, produced for the first time in the nation's history a uniform paper-money system.

The abolition of slavery and involuntary servitude was made final by the 13th Amendment, adopted in 1865. Two other amendments and the reconstruction policies of Congress were designed to assure the citizenship rights of the Negroes. The results were very limited, as were the efforts of the government through the Freedmen's Bureau to improve Negro education. Prior to the Civil War the economic and social structure of the South had hindered the development of free public education, especially in the rural areas. The rest of the nation thus pulled far ahead of the South in the movement for free public schools. Only slowly after the Civil War did southern state and local governments assume fuller responsibility for developing public school systems, particularly in rural areas and for the benefit of Negroes. From the Civil War until well into the twentieth century, private foundations worked on an increasing scale to help overcome these educational deficiencies in the South. This work provides an unusual case of voluntary organizations taking initiative in association with government to achieve institutional adjustments.

During the last three decades of the nineteenth century, basic economic problems multiplied while institutional adjustments lagged, especially those depending on governmental action. Except for the reconstruction measures, the policy changes occasioned by the Civil War were perpetuated. Tariff rates continued at high levels; and federal programs to promote agriculture, science, and inland and ocean navigation were expanded. Subsidies for the merchant marine became common. One innovation in promotional functions was federal appropriations to support state agricultural experiment stations. Another—of an organizational nature—was the creation in 1879 of the Geological Survey and the Coast and Geodetic Survey to regularize scientific survey work which the federal government had been conducting for about six decades.[5]

Monetary problems and controversies became very acute during this period. The clash between hard-money and soft-money views, which had occurred during colonial times and at both the state and federal level during the ante-bellum period, became more pronounced than ever after the Civil War. On the average, monetary policies had a deflationary effect in this period; and farmers for various reasons suffered low prices and financial ills. Advocacy of more greenbacks kept the Civil War greenbacks from being withdrawn from circulation. The free-silver advocates gained some coinage of silver during two intervals. However, government policy called for the resumption of specie payments, which was achieved by 1879. This hard-money action placed the United States on a *de facto* gold standard, which was formalized by law in 1900. The combined effect of these monetary policies, the National Banking System, and international financial conditions tended to depress the money supply and price levels. Several financial crises were brought on or worsened by the actions banks took when they lacked cash reserves. Except for the U.S. Treasury's willingness to pay out cash when banks desperately needed it, little was done by the government to reduce the instability inherent in the banking and fiscal systems or

[5] On the history of government and science in this country, see A. Hunter Dupree, *Science in the Federal Government* (Cambridge, Massachusetts: Belknap Press of Harvard University Press, 1957).

to avoid the deflationary effects of prevailing monetary policy. Relief from the latter fortunately ensued from the discovery of gold in Alaska and the increase of state-chartered banks, with their greatly expanded demand deposits, thanks to more lenient state regulatory law.

After the Civil War the regulatory activities of government began to increase, first on the state level and later the federal. At both levels the growth of public regulation of business was delayed by the tradition of laissez faire and the political ascendancy of businessmen. The effectiveness of regulatory measures was further retarded by the courts, which for many decades interpreted the concepts of property and contract and the due-process clauses in such a way as to make many regulatory activities seem confiscatory or unconstitutional. Adverse or restrictive court decisions greeted much of the early regulation of railroads and public utilities. The same was true for early social legislation in such areas as minimum wages, maximum hours, and working conditions. In like manner, the efforts of labor unions to organize and achieve collective bargaining were greatly hindered by court decisions stressing property rights of employers; and the courts frequently issued injunctions against unions. As interpreted by the courts, the legal rights of business remained strong while the legal status of public regulation and union activity was limited and precarious. These public and private efforts at institutional adjustment were as yet of limited import.

Throughout the nineteenth century most of the regulatory and social legislation continued to be state functions, as had been the tradition since the colonial period. After the Civil War when the beleaguered farmers wanted government regulation of railroads, grain elevators, and other middlemen to prohibit exorbitant and discriminatory charges, they naturally sought state regulation. In the 1870's and 1880's various states instituted such legislation, the first being the so-called "Granger laws" in the states of the Middle West. When the Supreme Court decided in 1886 that a state could not regulate rates on interstate shipments, the federal government was forced into its first major regulatory activity. In 1887 Congress passed the Interstate Commerce Act providing for railroad rate regulation through the Interstate Commerce Commission. The I.C.C. was hampered by court decisions and did not become very effective until further legislation was obtained early in the twentieth century.

The rapid development of "trusts" or business combinations led to demands for federal regulation to prevent business monopolies and conspiracies. No adequate relief had been gained through state legislation or through court action under common-law principles against conspiracies to restrain trade. In 1890 Congress passed the Sherman Antitrust Act, the second major federal regulatory measure. However, the act did little more than restate common-law rules; the courts limited its application; and efforts at enforcement were minimal for several years. The business combination movement proceeded apace. At the very time when the Sherman Act outlawed the trust device for combining, individual states were liberalizing their laws concerning the holding company, which was a more effective means of combination than the trust device. Although the Interstate Commerce and Sherman Acts were on the statute books, the federal government had hardly begun to regulate industry by the end of the nineteenth century.

In the period from 1900 to World War I, sometimes known as the Progressive Era, much new legislation was enacted. The role of the federal government increased accordingly. Legislative reform might have gone still further had it not been for the war. During the administration of Theodore Roosevelt the conservation movement began to influence legislation. The federal government took steps to protect forest reserves, to control floods, and to irrigate arid lands. Interest in the proper use of public power sites led to the Federal Power Act of 1920. Technical aid to agriculture was greatly expanded. Three acts between 1903 and 1910 increased the scope and effectiveness of the I.C.C. in railroad-rate regulation. Greater efforts were made to enforce the antitrust laws, and in 1911 the Supreme Court dissolved the Standard Oil Company and the American Tobacco Company. Then in 1914 Congress strengthened the antitrust program by passing the Clayton Act and an act creating the Federal Trade Commission. In that same year the Federal Reserve System was established. Other major changes under Woodrow Wilson included tariff reduction and introduction of the income tax using the principle of progressive rates.

World War I confronted the government with challenging problems of mobilization and war production. The war effort required new controls and a certain amount of planning. In the activities of the various war boards, industrialists and economists worked together. The former developed some notion about the possibilities of industrial cooperation, perhaps aided by government, as a means for solving common problems. The latter developed a high appreciation of the need for more economic statistics, and sometimes for more economic planning.[6] The war caused the government to organize its first system of employment exchanges, and it convinced industry as well as government of the inefficiencies caused by high turnover of labor. After transportation bottlenecks led the government to take over operation of the railroads, more efficient procedures were installed and perpetuated by railroad management. The absence of any planning for demobilization and reconversion was to be remembered, and corrected, in World War II. In short, the war greatly affected prevailing attitudes and practices concerning industry, government, and their relationships.

In contrast to the prewar years, the 1920's saw few major changes in government policy. One such change was of course the restriction of immigration. The tariff was increased at both the beginning and the end of this decade. Although there was a wave of business mergers, the antitrust laws were not very actively enforced; and the Supreme Court's famous "rule of reason" limited their applicability and effect. The government encouraged businessmen to hold trade-practices conferences, which strengthened the notion of industry self-regulation. In contrast to business combination, labor organizations encountered a shrinking membership. Unions were unable to organize the new mass-production industries; and employers had many effective weapons with which to oppose unions, including court injunctions and the yellow-dog contract, which the courts found constitutional. The farmers failed to obtain major legislative aid during the 1920's despite the agricultural depression running through this otherwise prosperous decade. However, the government began to subsidize the airlines with payments for carrying air mail.

The sweeping legislative changes and expanded role of government wrought by the depression and the New Deal in the 1930's are so well known that they need only to be noted here, to place them in historical context. In this context the depression indeed posed a grave emergency—even more grave than World War I—

[6] Wesley C. Mitchell was one of the economists who were greatly interested in economic planning from World War I on through the New Deal period. See my article, "Wesley Mitchell's Theory of Planning," *Political Science Quarterly* LXXII (March 1957), pp. 100–118.

and the New Deal's institutional adjustments were clearly revolutionary, even when compared to the changes occurring in the Hamiltonian era, the years following the War of 1812, or the Civil War decade. Although Wilson's New Freedom and Franklin Roosevelt's New Deal were separated by a geological fault produced by a war and postwar boom, these two reform eras had much in common. In some ways the New Deal took up where the New Freedom had left off, thus complementing and extending it. However, the complicated, pragmatic mixture of reform, recovery, and emergency-relief measures constituting the New Deal makes comparison and analysis very difficult. These three intermixed elements were accompanied by what was perhaps a fourth element, the effort to develop a workable scheme of planning and cooperation.

The New Deal legislative changes included a great deal of monetary and financial reform. The banking system was overhauled, and greater powers of monetary management were given to the Federal Reserve System. New agencies were created to protect bank depositors and holders of home and farm mortgages and corporate securities. New farm-credit programs were instituted, and the government entered the field of public housing. Significant changes were made in the tax system, and the Reciprocal Trade Agreements program was launched to reduce tariffs on a long-run basis. Public-utility regulation was developed in the fields of interstate transmission of electricity and natural gas, along with the control of holding companies in these fields. New social legislation included the Social-Security program, unemployment compensation, and wages-and-hours regulation—programs which originally had been pioneered by such states as Wisconsin. Farm-price supports and acreage limitations were made central to government aid for agriculture.

The National Recovery Administration provided an unusual experiment in industrial planning and stabilization. Although it failed in a general sense, it raised prices and wages, downgraded the concept of industry self-regulation, tested new forms of government regulation, and strengthened collective bargaining. It led to the Wagner Act creating the National Labor Relations Board and legitimatizing the institution of collective bargaining.[7] New Deal legislation thus strengthened the countervailing power of organized labor

[7] See Gardiner C. Means, *The Corporate Revolution in America* (New York: Crowell-Collier, 1962), pp. 33–37.

and even of the farmers in the modern industrial world of the giant corporation, the managerial revolution, and administered pricing.[8]

Among the chief developmental projects of the New Deal were the Tennessee Valley Authority and the Rural Electrification Administration. Although there were various public works and conservation programs, none was as significant as the T.V.A. with its unified planning approach for the development of a large river system. The example of the T.V.A. caused the regular governmental departments and agencies to evolve a more coordinated approach for planning and executing their various programs in other individual river valleys. Great stimulus was thus given to regional planning in this country. The National Resources Planning Board promoted the formation and coordinated the work of state and regional planning agencies. Many of them have survived as area development agencies, which now exist in great numbers and have been encouraged by such private organizations as the Committee for Economic Development and the National Planning Association. During the 1930's the National Resources Planning Board studied various problems of national as well as regional economic planning. One of these problems concerned the techniques for analyzing the relationships between production and consumption at various employment levels, including full employment. These techniques proved useful to the government during World War II in planning war production and making demobilization plans. This board studied the problem of demobilization planning until 1943, when it was abolished by Congress. The Committee for Economic Development used similar techniques in its wartime study of reconversion problems.[9]

The New Deal attacked the many problems of recovery and reform on a trial-and-error basis, with little benefit of systematic theory. Not much thought was given to the long-range effects of each program or the way these programs affected each other. The National Resources Planning Board no doubt grappled with these questions more than any other group. Although the early recovery measures were hasty, pragmatic efforts to meet a great emergency, the need for deficit spending during depression began to be grasped. The work of John Maynard Keynes, together with the impact of the 1937 recession, greatly clarified this understanding of contra-

[8] For example, see John Kenneth Galbraith, *American Capitalism: The Concept of Countervailing Power* (Boston: Houghton Mifflin, 1956).
[9] Means, *The Corporate Revolution*, pp. 185–191.

cyclical policy. The role of monetary and fiscal policy in an economic stabilization program came to be fairly well established. Although the New Deal brought acceptance of government responsibility for preventing unemployment, together with the requisite stabilization tools, it did not similarly establish the need for or the appropriate tools of general economic planning.

World War II brought far more wartime economic planning and controls than had World War I. Industrial priorities and direct controls of prices, wages, and consumer credit proved to be necessary. The wartime economy was essentially a controlled economy, with consumer rationing and similar restrictions on industrial consumption of productive resources. The level of economic performance was in such marked contrast to the depression that a firm resolve was formed to prevent postwar unemployment. Soon after the war began, various government agencies commenced to plan for the eventual personnel demobilization and economic reconversion. As noted above, the National Resources Planning Board worked on these problems until it was abolished in 1943, and the Committee for Economic Development studied means required to maintain full employment at war's end. This group challenged business leaders to make advance plans for postwar investment and to support the government's full-employment policy. During the war the "G.I. Bill" was enacted to aid returning veterans, and there was extensive discussion of a "full-employment bill" which eventuated in the Employment Act of 1946.

Some highlights of the postwar period may be briefly noted. In terms of broad economic policy, this period seems more or less continuous with the New Deal. The problems of full employment and economic stabilization have been foremost throughout this longer period. The Employment Act of 1946 underscored this central concern with stabilization policy. The act made clear the government's responsibility to maintain high-level employment, production, and income. Under this act, monetary and fiscal policy have remained the chief weapons of stabilization. The large postwar federal budgets and the management of a large public debt have been oriented to, and have usually aided, the purposes of stabilization. Other programs have commonly been administered, evaluated, and revised largely in terms of their effects on economic stability. All the major programs which survived the New Deal period have been continued, including farm-price supports, tariff reduction, public housing, and

wages-and-hours regulation. There have been extensions or enlarge-
ments of such programs as Social Security, unemployment compensation, and minimum wages.

Despite the basic continuity in economic policy from the New
Deal to the present, there have been significant changes in emphasis
among major problems and goals, along with several recent new
programs and reforms which may lead to a substantial reorientation
of policy. The postwar spiral of wage and price increases aroused
much concern about the problem of price stability. This problem
was seen to involve the hard realities of collective bargaining and
administered wages and prices. The impact of inflation on the competitive position of American industry in world trade and also on
the effectiveness of full-employment policy was recognized. Since
1958 the balance-of-payments deficits and the lagging growth rate
have become causes for concern. As a result, the problems of inflation, growth, and balance of payments have been given greater
weight than the drafters of the Employment Act may have contem-
plated. Furthermore, the unemployment rate rose to higher levels
at the very time these problems became more serious.

Many observers and policy makers have begun to feel that conventional "Keynesian" stabilization policy may not be able simultaneously to achieve the goals of price stability, full employment,
balance-of-payments equilibrium, and economic growth. New programs have been formulated to attack these problems, and many
new proposals have been advanced. Wage and price "guidelines"
have been developed to check inflation. These guidelines are essays
in exhortation or moral suasion. To succeed, they call for greater
commmunication and understanding among policy makers in government, industry, and labor. Perhaps this collective decision-making
can be better formalized and thus more informed, articulate, and
responsible. At the least, experience with the guidelines approach
may point the way toward more effective policy machinery. Proposals have been made for public hearings committees on proposed
price and wage increases in key industries and even for selective
price and wage controls in these areas. Clearly, government responsibility for price stability exceeds its present legal powers or instrumentalities.[10].

[10] For example, see Morris A. Copeland, *Our Free Enterprise Economy* (New
York: Macmillan, 1965), and Gardiner C. Means, *Pricing Power and the Public
Interest* (New York: Harper, 1962).

Several steps have been taken to meet the balance-of-payments difficulties. These include restrictions on government and tourist spending abroad and taxes and guidelines to discourage private loans and investments abroad. Here again, the technique of moral suasion is being tried, with some early show of promise. The government has also been promoting commodity exports in a variety of ways.

Great attention recently has been focused on the joint problems of excessive unemployment and low growth rates. Many new programs have been developed to promote business investment, area redevelopment, and "investment" in human resources. These programs have much the same pragmatic nature as early New Deal measures. They have a developmental and "structural" character that distinguishes them from orthodox stabilization policy. Thus, they may betoken a basic shift in policy, involving more reform or institutional adjustment and perhaps more planning. At any rate, a great deal of experimentation is in store as these new programs multiply.[11]

To encourage business investment, tax depreciation rules have been liberalized and tax laws have been changed, providing various investment credits and incentives. The government has been giving greatly increased support to area development, designed to encourage both public and private investment. In addition to urban renewal, public housing, and highway construction, these programs include the Area Redevelopment Act of 1961, the Trade Expansion Act of 1962 containing a provision to aid areas hurt by tariff reductions, and the Appalachian Regional Development Act of 1965. Similar stimulus to area development is involved in the Manpower Development and Training Act of 1962, the Higher Education Facilities Act of 1963, and the Economic Opportunity Act of 1964. Stimulus to business investment and area development is also provided in various other programs such as public works, conservation, atomic energy, scientific research and development, and education. Several of these recent programs are designed to improve human capital and its employability through health care, vocational education, retraining, and equal opportunity in employment. In addition to several of the acts already mentioned, these purposes are served by the Vocational Education Act of 1963, the Civil Rights Act of

[11] In several of his books Gunnar Myrdal has emphasized the problems and prospects of planning and structural change. For a challenging discussion of the role of law in social change, see Wolfgang Friedmann, *Law in a Changing Society* (Berkeley and Los Angeles: University of California Press, 1959).

1964, and the "Medicare" and various education acts passed in 1965.

The thrust of these new programs suggests that social reform and welfare may be converging with economic growth as major goals. The emphasis is on human capital, so called, as well as business investment, on greater employability as well as full employment, and on personal opportunity as well as aggregate economic performance. To achieve these joint goals may require greater time, resources, theoretical understanding, and systematic planning than is now recognized. However, these new programs suggest that the New Deal represented only a beginning, that the Keynesian revolution in economic policy may have to be given major new dimensions, and that the present era is by no means at an end with respect to the institutional adjustment now under way. The forward thrust of institutional change is dramatically indicated by such interacting developments as the desegregation and legislative redistricting decisions, the so-called Negro revolution, the new area-redevelopment programs, and the "war on poverty" program.

This historical review of the government's role in institutional adjustment indicates that the period from the New Deal to the present has been an era of unusual institutional change guided in a somewhat purposeful way by government. It also indicates, however, that there have been other such periods. These included the Revolution, the Hamiltonian era, the period following the War of 1812, the Civil War decade, and the Progressive Era through Wilson's administration. Between these more dynamic eras were times of compromise and consolidation, even stalemate and indecision. Such periods preceded the War of 1812 and the Civil War and then followed the Civil War and World War I. They gave way to eras of adjustment brought on by the shock of emergency such as war or depression and by renewed consensus as to national goals and the urgency of unsolved problems. This ebb and flow has kept institutions flexible, has called periodically for conscious long-range planning, and has continually augmented the role of government.

In the early national period the major tasks were to develop a basic institutional framework and to initiate economic growth. These tasks therefore involved a great deal of framework planning and developmental planning. Following the War of 1812 the urgent concern about the twin needs for defense and development triggered an unusual experiment with physical planning. The developmental function has continued to the present and has been greatly augmented, as in the fields of science, transportation, agriculture, and education. For several decades, however, the state governments were far more active in this promotional work than was the federal government. After the Civil War there were urgent demands for federal regulation of business, resulting especially from railroad-rate problems and the business-combination movement. The initial responses to those demands should not obscure the fact that the states had always regulated business or that federal regulation did not become very extensive or effective until the twentieth century.

The major shift in government functions in recent decades has been the assumption of responsibility to maintain full employment. This development of the New Deal period was intermixed with a good deal of institutional and social reform, with some attention to the need for planning. At the present time, institutional or structural change is again a very prominent consideration along with economic stabilization. Furthermore, this combination of institutional adjustment and stabilization policy—in the context of the pressing problems of growth, unemployment, depressed areas, international payments, administered inflation, and powerful private groups, as well as a welter of experimental new programs—may require that an orderly planning function be institutionalized to meet the challenges posed by our present national goals and immense economic potential.

W. FRIEDMANN

Creative Legal Interpretation and the Process of Institutional Adjustment

A CENTURY AND A HALF AGO, in emphasizing the role of law as a receptacle of slowly growing custom, the German jurist Friedrich von Savigny articulated what was then the prevailing approach to law. He bitterly opposed the rationalizing lawmaking of the French Revolution, which in turn corresponded to the thinking of Jeremy Bentham, an ardent advocate of rationalizing legislation as the appropriate instrument of social change. A century later Eugen Ehrlich, an Austrian jurist living under the racially and culturally heterogeneous Austro-Hungarian Empire, coined the phrase of the "living law." This was to him the embodiment of customs and practices observed in the life of the communities (notably in matters of family and personal relations) as distinct from state-made norms. He tended to restrict the sphere of the latter and to amplify that of the former.

The Law as Initiator

Half a century later the approach of Savigny, and even that of Ehrlich, seems remote. Even the most conservative of lawyers, even the most ardent enemy of official regulation of any sort, cannot deny that the law has, in contemporary society, an active, ubiquitous, and often creative function. This is simply a reflection of the state of contemporary urbanized and industrialized society, which for better or worse cannot let matters of social concern—from such basic issues as the desegregation of schools in the United States to such technical matters as the regulation of traffic—be controlled by the balance of "natural" social forces. The use of the legislative machinery—on both federal and state levels—for the implementation of new social policies and objectives, and for the creation of new institutions, has increased a hundredfold. But, perhaps more important for the purposes of this paper, the law now often serves as the initiator of new patterns of social behavior. This is particularly true where some basic changes in the structure of a society produce a modernizing trend in the law—expressed sometimes by a dictator, sometimes by an elite, sometimes by a new generation filling the key administrative and legislative posts—which clashes with traditional custom. Thus, in India the influence of Western ideas, as well as the need to transform India gradually from a status-bound country of village communities into a modern evolutionary and increasingly industrialized state, led to the legislative abolition of the caste system and polygamy. The authority and sanction of the law is used here to force a largely recalcitrant community into new patterns of behavior. That this is at best a slow and painful process, and at worst an overtaxing of the resources of law, is attested by much recent evidence on the persistence of old social customs, especially as regards the caste divisions. Again, modern legislation in a number of Moslem states emancipating women from their traditional status of inferiority and *apartheid* is the instrument chosen by modernizing political and social leaders—usually imbued with nationalist and socialist ideas —to transform traditional institutions and customs.

In most cases the interplay between evolution of social ideas and practices, and institutional adaptation through legislation, is more mutual and subtle. Thus, the labor legislation of the New Deal period, creating an institutional machinery for collective bargaining, both reflected and articulated the gradual rise in the status and acceptance of organized labor in contemporary American society. The creation of the institutional structure of labor relations boards, as a legislative cementing of the collective-bargaining processes, did, however, more than register an acceptance of organized labor and its methods of negotiation. It profoundly influenced the pattern of union organization and procedure.[1] Again, the Bonn Constitution

[1] In this respect the contrast with Britain—where the law interferes much less with the collective bargaining process—is illuminating.

of 1949, which established the principle of legal equality between men and women, articulated a new social philosophy that repudiated the traditional legal and social inferiority of the woman, especially of the married woman. But this constitutional provision in turn prompted many, as yet unfinished, changes in the law and practice of matrimonial property, the civic rights and public status of women, and others.

Examples could be multiplied. The machinery of the law, as one of the major social agents of any society, is now a far more active and important factor in social evolution than at any previous period in history.[2]

The most important single reason for the vast and continuing expansion of the function of law as an active moulder of social conditions, rather than a passive recipient, is the transition of contemporary society from laissez faire to regulation and from regulation to planning. To this corresponds the transformation of law from an essentially arbitral to a regulatory and from a regulatory to a directing function. Obviously these transitions are not clear-cut, nor are they equally marked in all contemporary societies, but the general phenomenon is beyond question. Even in the older and more settled societies—and those with a strong tradition of private investment and a free play of economic forces—the law increasingly fulfills the function of formulating policy goals and articulating a planned pattern of social evolution. An example to which Professor Eugene Rostow gives prominence in his book *Planning for Freedom* is the U. S. Employment Act of 1946, which declares it to be the obligation of the national government to use all its powers in order to create and maintain "conditions under which there will be afforded useful employment of opportunities, including self-employment, for those able, willing, and seeking to work, and to promote maximum employment, production, and purchasing power."

While the Employment Act creates no machinery for implementation but simply states national goals, the British Town and Country Planning Act of 1947, with subsequent amendments, does create new principles as well as new machinery for the use of land in the public interest. It establishes certain powers of expropriation,

---

[2] There have been, however, swings of the pendulum in previous centuries. The Tudor period in England, for example, was a far more active period of lawmaking than subsequent or previous periods in English history.

priorities, hearing procedures, and decision-making machinery to determine the use of land for certain public goals, such as the creation of new towns.

The directing function of law is greatly increased in the large number of new states (mainly Asian and African) which seek to build a modern society more or less from scratch. Here a series of laws are designed to create the institutional framework for the planned march of society, especially with respect to economic development. Some laws order the redistribution of land, often through radical interference with existing tribal and family custom, in order to construct public utilities, such as reservoirs, dams, or roads. Others lay down the general spheres of activities and priorities of both public and private enterprise, while investment laws regulate the place, priorities, privileges, and responsibilities of foreign investors within the framework of a national economic-development plan.

The Creative Function of Courts

The legislative process—that is, the creation of new types of social behavior or of new institutions through general norms, formulated in general codes or specific statutes, often implemented by administrative regulations—is not nearly sufficient to take care of the innumerable adjustments that occur in the fast-moving and densely organized society of our time. The legislator can handle only a limited number of cases, usually those that have major political or public-relations importance. Not only the so-called "lawyer's law" but many basic interpretations of general legislative norms must be left to the courts, or to quasi-judicial agencies entrusted with the application and interpretation of general norms.

The first point to stress is that the degree of leeway in the creativeness of judicial organs depends to a large extent on a) the political and constitutional system, b) the degree of generality of the norm in question.

The arbitral—and therefore creative—function of the judiciary is greatest in federal systems where the courts, or at least the supreme court of the country, play a decisive part in the allocation of functions between the federation and the member states. The impact of this role goes far beyond the strictly federal aspect (compare, for example, the relative competence of federal and state legislative powers). The interpretations of the court have a decisive effect on the scope of personal and economic liberties, on property rights, the structure of commerce, the educational and social service systems, and on many other fields.

No American need be reminded of the vital impact which the decisions of the United States Supreme Court have had on the basic economic and social structure of this country over many decades. A long line of decisions, which was finally reversed by a series of decisions commencing in 1936, invalidated for many decades the great majority of statutes which imposed modest standards with regard to maximum hours of work, minimum wages, or children's and women's labor, as unconstitutional interference with the freedom of contract (14th Amendment). Conversely, the decisions which have in the last few decades enlarged the meaning of the interstate-commerce clause, have had major impact not only on the flow of commerce within the United States, but on minimum standards of labor and social welfare in the great majority of services and products that transcend the frontiers of any one state.

Such decisive effects of judicial interpretations are paralleled in other federations. Thus, some fifteen years ago the High Court of Australia invalidated a statute passed by the then incumbent Labor Government, which, under an apparently clear federal competence to legislate in matters of banking, purported to nationalize the banks. The Judicial Committee of the Privy Council, until recently the highest court for Canada, in a series of decisions invalidated the Canadian "New Deal" legislation by reference to a section of the British-North America Act. More recently, the High Court of India has exercised a profound influence on the redistribution of land in India by its decisions on the adequacy of compensation for expropriation of land in the public interest—a decision subsequently restricted by a constitutional amendment. The Federal Supreme Court of Western Germany has influenced the meaning of the provisions on equality of sexes by its interpretations of the relevant provisions of matrimonial property law.

That the decision of a court can have an epoch-making influence on the whole social structure of a country has recently been demonstrated by the direct and indirect impact of the decision of the Supreme Court in *Brown* vs. *Board of Education,* 1954 (school desegregation). This decision, based on a constitutional provision of general impact, set in train a whole series of events, the final effect of which cannot yet be foreseen. The school desegregation decision, and other decisions of a similar character produced a whole series

of judicial and administrative adjustments in the majority of states
that, more or less willingly, complied with the decision, while it set
in train a swelling protest movement in the minority of states which
failed to comply. Not only in the field of education, but in those of
transport, communications, voting rights, and other areas, the decision of the Court sparked and legitimated wide-ranging protest
movements which in turn produced in 1964 the Civil Rights Act, and
in 1965 further legislation designed to make equality of voting for
Negroes a reality rather than a paper provision. We have here a
fascinating and important interplay between constitution, creative
judicial interpretation, and statutory consolidation. The Constitution
provides a broad framework of basic political principles which differ
from those of a political declaration in that they are accepted as
the basic law of the country. But they leave such a wide scope of
differing social and economic philosophies that they are reinterpreted
from generation to generation, often in sweeping manner. After a
long period of quiescence, marked by such decisions as *Plessy* vs.
Ferguson ("separate but equal doctrine"), the *Brown* decision became, in effect, the starting point for a new era in the ordering of
social relations. But as judicial decisions in matters of education,
voting district apportionment, provision of legal aid, and many
other matters can only lay down the basic principles, they must
sooner or later lead to detailed regulation, which will provide the
necesssary institutional and administrative framework to implement
the principles of the creative decision.

The realization of the inevitable limitations in creativity which
result from the very nature of the judicial process—the *ad hoc* decision on a specific issue between individuals, states, public authorities, or corporations—could provide some insight into the delimita-
tion of spheres of creativity, as between legislator and courts. I have
suggested elsewhere[3] that

> Courts can and indeed are called upon to adjust rights and liabilities in
> accordance with changing canons of public policy. But because they de-
> velop the law on a case-by-case basis they cannot, as can the legislature,
> undertake the establishment of a new legal institution, "an elaborate pro-

---

[3] See, for example, W. Friedmann, *Legal Philosophy and Judicial Law Making,*
61 Columbia Law Review 821 (1961), reprinted in *Essays on Jurisprudence
from the Columbia Law Review* (New York: Columbia University Press, 1963),
pp. 101 ff.

cedure of investigation and consideration eventuating in the approval of a particular form of words as law."[4]

As has already been mentioned, the striking down of the various discriminatory legal practices regarding Negroes as a matter of general principle must be followed up by an institutional adjustment which can only be provided by legislation. When the German courts, a decade or so ago, were called upon to implement the constitutional principle of equality between the sexes, during an interregnum when the old provisions of the civil code had been declared invalid in the Constitution but a new statute had not yet been passed, they laid down the principle of separation of property as the one nearest the constitutional principle. But this broad interpretation of principle had to be followed up—as it was—by a statute which laid down in detail the intricate apportionment and accounting procedures between the properties and incomes of husband and wives. The Supreme Court decision in *Baker* vs. *Carr,* which commanded the reapportionment of voting districts so as to implement the principle of equality, must be followed up by the appropriate federal and state laws redrawing and providing the appropriate administrative machinery for the redistricting on the basis of the new principle.

There are, of course, borderline cases. Some years ago the English courts were much perturbed by the plight of English war brides who had married American or other foreign servicemen during the war and found themselves subsequently deserted. Normally, the legal title in the matrimonial home would be vested in the husband —who, in this case, could often not be found. The English Court of Appeal in 1952 proclaimed a "new equity," namely the right of the deserted wife to continue occupancy of the matrimonial home, in face of the absence of any property or joint-tenancy rights on her part.[5] But property lawyers objected to the vagueness of this new right, and to the difficulty of classifying it among the recognized and registrable property interests.[6] The Court subsequently modi-

---

[4] Comment by Henry M. Hart, Jr., in Monrad G. Paulsen (ed.), *Legal Institutions Today and Tomorrow* (New York: Columbia University Press, 1959), p. 46.

[5] *Bendall* vs. *McWhirter* [1952] 2 Q.B. 466.

[6] The Court of Appeal's decision in *Bendall* vs. *McWhirter,* even in its modified form, was recently overruled by the House of Lords in *National Provincial Bank* vs. *Ainsworth* [1965] 2 AER 472. Much of the criticism of the House of Lords was directed against judicial invention of "an equity" detached from an estate or interest in land, and yet supposed to be binding on third persons.

fied its doctrine so as to strip the new right of its quasi-property character and to turn it into a personal equity vis-à-vis third parties who had actual or constructive knowledge of the position.

There has been much debate whether it is appropriate for the American law courts to abolish the antiquated and inequitable doctrine of "contributory negligence," under which the slightest negligence on the part of the plaintiff—for example, in motor car accidents—defeats his claim despite overwhelming fault on the part of the defendant. The obvious substitute is "comparative negligence," an apportionment of claims according to the respective degree of fault. But this has considerable effect on the insurance rates, which today dominate in fact though not in theory this part of the law of negligence.

What this brief survey shows is that the courts have and do exercise a vital function in formulating new basic principles, which sometimes can stand by themselves—insofar as they regulate rights and liabilities—but which normally will call for subsequent legislative and administrative action to give them precise institutional shape. A court may respond to changing standards of public policy, for example, by reinterpreting wills so as to include illegitimate children in the testator's use of the word "children." But they must leave it to the legislator to modify the general status of illegitimate children, or to create new institutions of family law such as legitimation or adoption.

The range of creativeness is usually dependent on the degree of generality of the underlying constitutional or statutory provisions. There is a great difference between the American Constitution and the interpretation of a bankruptcy act. But it would be quite wrong to conclude that only general, deliberately policy-making legislative instruments, such as constitutions or other basic statutes, yield to constructive judicial interpretation. Quite often an apparently technical statute can become the point of departure for decisions of wide-ranging social implications. Thus, the U.S. Supreme Court, in 1960, in *United States* vs. *Republic Steel Corporation*[7] was called upon to interpret the term "obstruction" used in the Rivers and Harbors Act of 1890, which specifically defines a number of structures or activities constituting "obstruction." The question was whether the depositing of industrial wastes in suspension in a navigable river

[7] 362 U.S. 482 (1960).

constituted such an obstruction. This was a matter of no consequence, and clearly not foreseen, in 1890, but one of vital importance in 1960, (and even more so in 1965). The Court held by a bare majority that the broad purpose of the act was the safeguarding of navigation and commerce in the vital waterway. The majority opinion was strongly attacked by the minority as reading into the statute things that were not there, in order to achieve a socially desirable purpose.

There is thus a whole range of judicial creativeness, often the starting point for sweeping institutional readjustments and ranging from broad constitutional provisions to apparently technical clauses of specific statutes.

A parallel process takes place in the interpretation of precedent. As Justice Breitel has observed: "the law making role of courts is not determined primarily by whether stated principles or rules of law are statutory or decisional in origin."[8] It is the techniques rather than the principles that are different. A court that interprets precedents rather than statutes must exercise its creativity through the reinterpretation of precedent. This it can do either by the distinction of facts or the selection of one *ratio decidendi* rather than another, or the manipulation with obiter dicta and individual judgments in a collective decision. The techniques are manifold and have been analyzed time and again by jurists of many countries.

The extent to which courts have used this freedom has differed from time to time, and it is greatly influenced not only by the prevailing legal philosophy of the time but even more by the inclinations of judges. That the scope for judicial lawmaking, with far-reaching social and institutional implications, is very great indeed may be illustrated by two situations, both of them the subject of very recent decisions by Britain's highest court, the House of Lords. These are chosen not only because the problems decided by the House of Lords are of great social and economic importance to the United States, but also because the House of Lords, unlike the American Supreme Court, professes to be strictly bound by its own precedent and because the prevailing English judicial philosophy leans far more strongly than that of their American brethren towards judicial self-limitation.

Until a generation ago it was accepted doctrine both in England

---

[8] Charles D. Breitel, "The Courts and Law Making," in Paulsen (ed.), *Legal Institutions Today and Tomorrow*, p. 21.

and the United States, that a manufacturer could be held liable in negligence—for example, in the manufacture of a gun, a food product, or an automobile—only to his immediate purchaser, but not to the ultimate consumer. This was based on the doctrine of privity of contract and the deduction that A, if liable in contract to B, could not simultaneously be liable outside contract to C. This doctrine was reversed first in the United States in 1916 and then in Britain in 1932, as a result of radical transformation of the relationship between producer and consumer. Users of motor cars as well as consumers of food products could no longer be equitably restricted to recourse against the wholesaler or retailer who is nowadays merely a conduit pipe for mass-manufactured products. But then the further question arose whether this new doctrine, should be applied to statements made by professional people, with reference to financial investment or other commercial decisions. Could an accountant or a bank be held liable for a negligent statement or opinion on the creditworthiness of an enterprise to one whose reliance on such statement caused him financial loss? Both American and British courts have until very recently denied this further extension of the new doctrine. But in 1963 the House of Lords unanimously established a new doctrine.[9] In substance it is that there may be legal responsibility for statements or information given by a person professionally or commercially qualified to do so, to somebody who may be expected to rely on it, in circumstances of a contractual or near-contractual relationship. Although the authority of the decision may be questioned on the ground that, in the case at hand, the defendant bank had specifically disclaimed responsibility for its statement and that such disclaimer was held to be admissible, it is likely to be regarded as authoritative. This may give a totally new dimension to the insurability as well as to the rates of insurance for activities not hitherto covered by the customary insurance policies.

An even more dramatic illustration of the power of court to reverse a long-established policy trend is provided by the very recent decision of the House of Lords in *Rookes* vs. *Barnard*.[10] This dealt with a matter vital to the relations between organized labor and employers. An employee of the BOAC, who had left the union, sued

[9] *Hedley Byrne* vs. *Heller* [1963] 3 W.L.R. 101.
[10] [1964] 2 W.L.R. 269.

two fellow employees and a union organizer who was not an employee, for having instigated the BOAC to terminate his employment (without any breach of contract). The union had threatened to strike, despite a nonstrike clause in their collective agreement with the BOAC, unless the plaintiff was dismissed. The decision of the House unanimously held the three defendants liable in damages to the plaintiff. Half a century ago the English courts had tended to consider boycott actions by a union—therefore, in view of the unincorporated status of unions, the organizers—to be an actionable conspiracy. But gradually, culminating in a House of Lord's decision in 1942,[11] the courts had come to recognize lockout, boycotts, and strikes as legitimate means of collective pressure. Moreover, the Trade Disputes Act of 1906—which was a deliberate reaction to an earlier decision of the House of Lords—had specifically declared any action done in pursuance of an agreement or combination to be "'not actionable unless the act if done without any such agreement or combination would be actionable." It furthermore declared that an act "shall not be actionable on the ground only that it induces some other person to break the contract or employment or that it is an interference with the trade, business or employment of some other person, or with the right of some other person to dispose of his capital or his labor as he wills."

In order to hold the organizers in the present action liable, the House, in the words of an authoritative commentator,[12] "invented a new extension of civil liability and then reduced to insignificance the protections of the Trade Dispute Act of 1906 which should have been a defense against it." The House unearthed an almost forgotten tort of "intimidation," the existence of which was doubted by many authorities on the law of tort, in order to circumvent the application of the act. But even if such a tort exists, the decision bristles with technical difficulties and has met with severe criticism on the part of most commentators. The reason for the decision—even though it does not make the slightest reference to the social policy issues— is unquestionably the greatly strengthened position of trade unions, and a reaction, in the courts and a substantial segment of public opinion, against the frequency of strikes interrupting vital services, as well as against the dictatorial habit of some union officials.

[11] *Crofter Handwoven Harris Tweed Co.* vs. *Veitch* [1942] A. C. 435.
[12] K. W. Wedderburn, *Intimidation and the Right to Strike*, 27 Modern L.R. 257 (1964).

Even those who support the decision cannot deny that it requires a remarkable degree of legal acrobatics to arrive at it. The consequences of the decision may be many. Trade unions are likely to refrain from "no strike" clauses in future collective bargaining, thus making the entire process more complex. The Labor Government has initiated legislation to reverse the decision. Any legislation designed to reverse a particular court decision is always unfortunate since it undermines confidence in the authority of the judicial branch of government.[13] It is thus as important for law courts to appraise wisely the need for a judicial adaptation of inequitable and outmoded doctrines as it is to be aware of the limitations. It is the fear of political repercussions of decisions that are too policy-minded and not sufficiently "principle-minded" that has led Herbert Wechsler, to proclaim "principled neutrality" as the best guide to constitutional interpretation.[14] But this doctrine also has its severe limitations since almost any decision implies a choice between conflicting values—for instance, between the principle of racial equality and the principle of freedom of contract and association (in the so-called Caucasian covenants used in many land purchases).

In conclusion, it is no easier to give a clear-cut answer to the question how far courts should go in creativity than to many other questions of life, which is a difficult business implying painful choices. Three points, I hope, have emerged from the preceding discussion. a) The creative part of courts in the adaptation of law to new social conditions and changing values is inevitable as well as necessary. b) Interaction between the lawmaking and the courts, by which sometimes the one and sometimes the other initiates a new principle, is a necessity. Where the legislator takes the initiative, it falls to the court to implement and articulate the statutory norms by interpretations that bear out the policy of the statute but make it as consistent as possible. Where the court takes the initiative, it can generally only give certain guide-lines to be followed up by the legislator in the specific creation of a new status, a new administrative or other institutional arrangement. c) The courts must

---

[13] This applies to the recent hasty Congressional action in reversing the effect of the Supreme Court decision in a very important matter of international law, in the so-called Sabbatino case, or to the repeated but hitherto unsuccessful attempts made in Congress to reverse the ruling in the apportionment cases.

[14] "Toward Neutral Principles of Constitutional Law," in Herbert Wechsler, *Principles, Politics and Fundamental Law* (Cambridge, Massachusetts: Harvard University Press, 1961), pp. 3 *et seq.*

have a particularly fine sense of the possible. They can neither run too far ahead of the prevailing consensus of public opinion nor limp too far behind it. Within these limits there is much scope for many shades between boldness and timidity. The Supreme Court in the school desegregation decision took a bold step but one which it rightly judged was sufficiently in accord with the development of American public philosophy to set the trend for the next few decades, despite much procrastination and defiance. Half a century earlier, such a decision would probably have remained a cry in the wilderness.

MORRIS A. COPELAND

Implementing the Objective
of Full Employment in Our
Free Enterprise Economy

As World War II drew to a close in 1945, many people, mindful of their experiences during the 1930's, were deeply concerned about the possibility of severe postwar unemployment. But the business recession of 1945 proved to be very mild. Hence about the only action taken at the time was the passage of the Employment Act of 1946. That made full employment an official objective of federal government policy, but it provided no real implementation for this objective. Nor have we done much to implement this objective since.[1]

Present Policy and Cycle Prospects

During the past seven years we have had an unemployment level that in 1946 was widely considered to be intolerably high. In each of those seven years on the average 5.2 per cent or more of the members of our civilian labor force were unemployed. We have, indeed, taken various steps to alleviate this situation. But it cannot be said that these steps were particularly prompt, or that they have been clearly adequate.[2]

Some of us have suffered because of unemployment. But most of us, most of the time since World War II, have been very prosperous.

---

[1] The writer is grateful to three of his colleagues, Alfred E. Kahn, Robert W. Kilpatrick, and George J. Staller, for helpful suggestions and criticisms.

[2] During 1965 the unemployment rate decreased somewhat. The average rate for the year was 4.6 per cent.

And a number of us have become decidedly complacent about the problems of inadequate aggregate demand.

During the 1930's various changes were made in the financial structure of our economy that greatly strengthened it. And since that time federal government receipts and expenditures have come to behave in a way that tends appreciably to dampen cyclical fluctuations in our GNP. Some people, impressed by the high level of business activity that on the whole has prevailed during the past twenty years and by this built-in fiscal cycle dampener, have come to think that the business cycle has become permanently milder, that we could never again have a major prolonged business contraction. To those who think this way I would call attention to a possible historical parallel. During the New Era that preceded the 1929 stock market crash, two of the then leading economists made statements indicating that they thought the business cycle had grown milder. History could repeat itself.

Quite a number of people today advance another ground for believing we will never have another really serious and prolonged cyclical downswing. They cite what we have learned about the subject of macroeconomics. They claim that we now know how to manage our GNP and that we would never let it take another nose dive. But the policy we have been following refutes this claim. That policy has been to rely on our built-in cycle dampener and on countercyclical monetary and credit policy most of the time, and to take special steps appropriate for particular situations only as and when they occur. For a major recession this means waiting until it occurs. In fact, it means waiting during a recession until the decrease in business activity is so large that the recession is clearly a major one, and then waiting some more while the Congress decides what action to take. In other words, we would let our GNP take another nose dive before action to deal with the situation could possibly become effective.

But is there any real prospect of another major business recession? Do not the improvements in our financial structure plus our built-in cycle dampener plus our countercyclical monetary and credit policy make a really deep contraction extremely unlikely? Our monetary and credit policy is not very pertinent here. While tight credit can put on the brakes during a cyclical upswing, easy credit cannot really halt a downswing. The contrast between what our monetary and credit authorities can do to check an expansion in business activity and what they can do to induce one is explained in the much used metaphor, "you cannot push on a string." And as for the improvements in our financial structure and our built-in cycle dampener, they do something to reduce the extent to which a cyclical contraction is cumulative and self-accelerating, but the main basis for the cumulative nature of the contraction still remains. It is still true that a decrease in any one component of aggregate demand makes for subsequent decreases in other components. Moreover, an important reason why we have cyclical contractions in business activity is that different parties purchase different parts of our national product, and that each party is free to decide either to decrease or to increase his purchases. We have done nothing of consequence that would prevent a contraction of those purchases of national product that have been most prominent in past cyclical downswings, the purchases of new durable goods and the outlays on new private construction.

The addition of a built-in cycle dampener to our fiscal operations and the strengthening of our financial structure are developments that tend to moderate cyclical contractions. But they are not the only developments to be considered. Business cycles involve other countries as well as the United States. The 1929–1933 debacle may have started here, but it was definitely international, and the length and amplitude of this business contraction were in large part due to the fact that most of the world participated in it. Since 1929 a larger and larger part of world production has been getting to be production for a market. This development has meant an increased interdependence of national economies, an interdependence which in turn has probably substantially enhanced the chances of another major worldwide business depression.

The Requirements of an Adequate Program

I think we should take whatever steps may be needed to implement the full-employment objective of the Employment Act of 1946, but I shall not here attempt to argue the case for doing so. Instead I shall assume it. I should like to show that we can adequately implement that full-employment objective under our free enterprise system. I intend to try to do this by suggesting a possible program.

But let me make clear at the outset what I take the full-employment objective to mean. It does not mean completely eliminating unemployment. We usually assume today that one part of unemployment is due to the inadequate level of aggregate demand, and that the rest of it is what is called frictional. Frictional unemployment includes between-job unemployment—there are always a certain number of people who have left one job and not yet started on another. It also includes seasonal unemployment, and structural-change unemployment—unemployment that results from technological innovations like automation and from other changes that make particular jobs in particular places no longer needed. Full employment has been commonly taken to mean the elimination only of the part of unemployment that is due to the business cycle and to inadequate aggregate demand. That is what I shall mean by the term.

Frictional unemployment is a serious problem. I had originally hoped to include it in my paper and to discuss what can be done to alleviate the suffering it causes and what can be done to reduce it. But within the time at my disposal that does not seem possible.

There are two other topics to which I should have liked to give attention, but which I have decided to by-pass: These are proposals to deal with the problems of unemployment by shortening the working week, and proposals to deal with these problems by shortening the working life of the average worker. As a time-saving expedient I shall take existing practices regarding working weeks and working lives as given. By full employment, then, I mean a situation in which, under existing working-time practices, our economy is operating substantially at full capacity.

To deal with the high level of unemployment we have had in the last several years there have been various proposals for adult education and for vocational training for the relatively unskilled part of our labor force. Certainly such education and such training are desirable. And there are presumably some job vacancies at the present level of aggregate demand that will be filled if and when suitable candidates become available. But for the most part improving the education and training of our working force is not properly a remedy for excessive unemployment. Raising the level of competence of potential workers is doubtless a laudable objective. But it may in effect add to our labor supply. And our unemployment problem is primarily a problem of inadequate demand, not of inadequate supply. I do not plan to discuss what should be done by way of adult education and vocational training.

To implement the objective of full employment we should adopt measures that will keep our economy operating at a full-capacity level, measures that will eliminate unemployment to the extent that unemployment is due to the inadequacy of aggregate demand. I believe we should adopt such measures. But I think there are certain requirements these measures should meet. They should emphasize the role of consumers' free choice in determining the composition of our national product, and they should improve and not hamper the efficiency with which our free enterprise system operates. Therefore the measures we take should in general work through price and cost relationships and leave the composition of our national product—at any rate its long-run average composition—and the apportionment of our resources to be determined by the profit system and by market adjustments. Just what this means will be clearer as we consider the various measures that might be parts of a full-employment program.

However, one kind of development that it is urgent to avoid had best be noted now. It is easy to conceive a level of aggregate demand that is too high. We had such a level during both world wars. And with it came demand pressures that gave a strong impetus to both price increases and wage increases. The increases were kept in bounds by wartime price and wage controls. Even in peacetime we have a little in the way of controls; for example, a federal minimum-wage law, and an agricultural price-support program. But we do not want the general price and wage controls we thought necessary during the wars. They would, if imposed permanently in peacetime, be substantial abrogations of our free enterprise system. Certainly a full-employment program should avoid raising aggregate demand to a level that would create the need for general price and wage controls.

The measures we adopt to implement the full-employment objective should be measures that avoid the threat of what is called galloping inflation. But we cannot avoid inflation altogether. We have not done so, even though we have not had full employment. Ever since the business upswing that began early in 1933, the GNP price index has been higher at the end of every business cycle than at its beginning. Even if we confine our attention to the past decade we have had gradually increasing prices—what is called creeping inflation. Creeping inflation seems to be a feature of our present economy.

It should be possible to devise a full-employment plan that would avoid galloping inflation, but it could not be expected to avoid creeping inflation. In fact it would almost certainly slightly accelerate the year-to-year rate of price increases. However, the problems of the gradual upward trend of prices would not be much more serious than they have been during the past several years. And whatever else may be said about them, they do not seem to call for price and wage controls. They are not our present concern.

To implement the full-employment objective we must have measures that are capable of bringing about an increase in aggregate demand, if an increase is needed to raise the national product to capacity level. But they must also be capable of checking any further demand increase and even of reducing demand, if a check or reduction is needed to avoid strong inflationary pressures. We must have measures that will provide both stimulants and restraints, strong enough stimulants to assure full employment, strong enough restraints to prevent over-full employment.

But this is not all. For the adequate implementation of the full-employment objective, there is a time requirement. It should be possible to shift from stimulants to restraints, or from restraints to stimulants, or to strengthen or to weaken either the stimulants or the restraints, as circumstances seem to indicate. And it should be possible to make such shifts promptly. To be adequate the implementation must make possible what has been called a steering-wheel approach, that is to say, an approach under which the level of aggregate demand will be continuously adjusted—the stimulation strengthened or weakened, or the restraints weakened or strengthened—so that the economy will always be operating at a level that is close to its capacity, but never at a level that seriously taxes its capacity.

Let us consider how such a full-employment program would operate, assuming that adjustments can be made in its various parts for each quarter before the beginning of the quarter, and that these adjustments are made on the basis of rough estimates of the amounts of change in aggregate demand that will result. Somewhat ahead of time the production objective for each quarter should have been established—the amount of total GNP and of each major component, private-capital formation, personal consumption expenditure, and so forth, to be aimed at. Shortly before the beginning of each quarter the first step in determining the adjustments will be to estimate aggregate demand on the assumption that no change is to be made from the previous quarter to strengthen or weaken either stimulants or restraints. This estimate will make clear the sort of program changes, if any, that are needed.

If the no-change-in-stimulation estimate of GNP is greater than the objective, to avoid undesirable inflationary pressures the intensities of restraints must be increased and the intensities of stimuli decreased. If the estimate of GNP is less than the objective, changes must be made in the opposite direction. How big the changes should be will necessarily be a matter of judgment. But clearly such adjustments can be expected to improve as those responsible for making them gain experience with the operation of the program. And it is of the essence of the steering-wheel approach that errors in determining the adjustments for any quarter can be compensated for three months later.

The program that I want to submit for your consideration contains four parts. Part I is a buffer stock proposal; Part II a proposal for a works-projects shelf. Both these parts would provide countercyclical demand influences. Part III is a proposal for reducing the cyclical fluctuations in construction activity and in the purchases of producers' and consumers' durable goods. Part IV is designed to deal with the problem of a secular deficiency in aggregate demand. These four proposals certainly do not exhaust all the promising possibilities that might help to promote a full-employment program. They do fit together so as to meet the requirements of the steering-wheel approach for quarterly changes in the stimuli and the restraints, and together their influences should be strong enough to provide adequate implementation of the full-employment objective.

PART I. A BUFFER STOCK PROPOSAL

The first proposal I want to offer for your consideration is a particular form of buffer stock operation, an operation that would considerably reduce the cyclical ups and downs of the prices of the commodities it covers and the ups and downs in the incomes of the people engaged in producing these commodities. The commodities would be staples, farm products and raw materials that could be stored for as much as a year without undue spoilage or deterioration.

A buffer stock operation requires the establishment of an enterprise that will be on the demand side of a market when the market is weak and on the supply side when the market is strong. Let us assume such an enterprise and refer to it as the Stabilization Corporation.

My proposal is for a buffer stock operation that covers a number of commodities, but it will be convenient for a moment to assume the Stabilization Corporation covers only one. Let us say it is cotton. Under the kind of operation I assume, the Stabilization Corporation will announce for each market in which it operates a support price for cotton. At this price it will buy all the cotton that is offered. Also the Corporation will announce a higher ceiling price at which it will sell whatever part of its inventory may be demanded. If the support and ceiling prices are properly set, in each market in which the Corporation operates the price will fluctuate between them.

There are difficult problems in setting the right support and ceiling prices, and in revising them when changed supply and demand conditions require revisions. And there are other difficult problems, too. If they can be solved, a buffer stock operation covering a number of commodities has much to commend it. The spreads between support and ceiling prices could be wide enough to cover the operating costs of the Stabilization Corporation and still substantially reduce the price fluctuations to which a good many staples have been subject in the past. The Corporation could be an international enterprise that operates in world markets. It should be. It could be financed by getting participating countries to subscribe to its capital stock.

I shall not here attempt to go into most of the problems such a buffer stock operation would involve. I shall simply assume that they are soluble. But I want to take up very briefly the principal problem, that of fixing the prices.

In general the producers of any commodity that is to be included in a stabilization arrangement are more vocally interested than the consumers. Hence there has been a tendency to make the arrangement aim at valorization rather than stabilization, that is, at increasing the average level of prices. The result has often been difficulties in a firm policy for the liquidation of stocks when the market situation seems to call for it.

There is no way to make the producers and consumers equally vocal, but some years ago Benjamin Graham suggested a plan that takes the edge off the difference in pressures from the two sides of the market so that it is much easier to handle.[3] In effect his plan—or rather the part of it that is pertinent here—is that our Stabilization Corporation shall fix, not the price of any individual commodity, but a price index of all the commodities covered by the arrangement. Under Graham's plan the stabilization agency undertakes to buy and sell, not the individual commodities, but what he calls commodity

[3] Benjamin Graham, *World Commodities and World Currency* (New York: McGraw-Hill, 1944).

bales. Each bale would represent title to a particular bill of goods —a specified number of bushels of wheat, a specified number of tons of pig tin, a specified number of pounds of coffee, and so on. Purchases of multiple amounts of this bill of goods—ten bales, one hundred bales, or whatever the market would supply at the Stabilization Corporation's announced support price—would keep the price of the bale in the markets in which the Corporation operates, from falling below this price. And once the Corporation had acquired title to a substantial number of bales, sales from its inventory at its announced ceiling price would keep the price of a bale from rising above this figure. The price of the bale would be pegged between these limits, but the price of each commodity in the bale would be free to fluctuate within a fairly wide range in response to changes in the demand for and supply of it. This is one of the advantages of the Graham plan. While it permits supply-and-demand adjustments in each individual market, a large part of the approximately synchronous ups and downs in the prices of the various covered commodities in response to the business cycle would be ironed out. The second advantage is that it should be easier to stick to the announced selling price for the bale than it would be to stick to a separate announced selling price for each of the commodities. And there is a third advantage in fixing the Corporation's buying and selling prices. If the buying and selling prices of each commodity were to be determined separately on the basis of an analysis of its market prospects, some of these prices would be too high, others too low. In determining the prices for the bale, the "Law of Large Numbers" would operate. Because of offsetting errors it should be possible to do a significantly better job in fixing the prices for the bale than in setting separate prices for the commodities included in it.

Part II. A Works-Project Shelf Proposal

Part I of the full-employment program I offer, then, is a buffer stock Stabilization Corporation along the lines suggested by Benjamin Graham. It would provide a kind of demand counter-cycle. As Part II of my full-employment program I shall take another kind of demand countercycle. I propose a public-works shelf and the establishment of a federal agency to operate it. I shall call the agency the Shelf Projects Administration.

The idea that public works could provide a component of aggregate demand that would increase when business is poor and decrease when business is brisk is very appealing. But a major difficulty with this idea has been that for most construction projects the preliminary steps that must be taken before they can get underway are too time-consuming. A project must be authorized, the detailed plans agreed upon, the funds appropriated, and the contracts let; and there may be still other preliminary steps. All told these steps may take well over a year. Because they take so long it is easy to imagine that an effort made during a business downswing to get a substantial number of projects started might increase the volume of public construction, not during the downswing, but rather during the ensuing business upswing. A major difficulty with the idea of a works-projects counter-cycle is the difficulty of managing the timing of the projects so that they will help and not aggravate the business cycle.

Some years ago I made a suggestion for getting around the difficulty that I should now like to explain briefly.[4] To begin with let me note two conditions that must be met if we are to have an effective works-projects shelf. Condition Number 1 is that there must be some way to put projects on the shelf. Condition Number 2 is that there must be some way to take them off. There are today many billions of dollars worth of needed public-works projects that we ought to be willing to undertake. But that does not mean we have a works shelf. We have done nothing as yet to establish procedures for putting any project on the shelf or for taking it off.

To arrange for the operation of the shelf I propose that the Shelf Projects Administration get every agency that is willing to sponsor a shelf project to enter into an agreement that will give the Administration control over the timing of projects. Each agreement should provide, first, that the project sponsor will defer the operation of his project until he receives notice from the Shelf Projects Administration to activate it, and, second, that he will activate his project promptly on receipt of such notice.

To make project agreements into propositions that would be attractive to state and local government agencies and probably also to some private agencies, I propose that the Shelf Projects Administration offer them suitable money inducements.

To make it possible for the Shelf Projects Administration to in-

<hr/>

[4] Morris A. Copeland, "Business Stabilization by Agreement," *American Economic Review*, XXXIV (June 1944), 328–339.

crease the amount of shelf-projects work in process reasonably promptly I propose that the Administration impose on the prospective project sponsor as a condition for entering into an agreement a readiness-to-go requirement. So far as possible all the necessary time-consuming preliminary steps should have been taken before a project would be accepted for inclusion in the shelf.

The Shelf Projects Administration on its part should agree to definite limits on project deferments. For some projects the maximum deferment period might be two years; for others, three years or possibly more. The bonus offered to make project agreements attractive to non-federal-government sponsors should be larger for projects subject to a longer deferment period.

Proposals for a works-projects shelf have often been restricted to public-construction projects. Experience with the WPA and other programs during the 1930's makes clear that they should not be restricted to construction projects. And there is no reason for requiring sponsors to be government agencies. The terms of project agreements could be such that some private businesses and quite possibly also private research agencies would find them attractive.

There should be only three primary conditions for including a project in the shelf. (1) The project should be ready to go; (2) the sponsor should agree to its deferment; and (3) he should agree to activate it promptly on receipt of his activation notice.

I say only three conditions. The Shelf Projects Administration should have no part in determining the merits of the projects included in the shelf. Any government agency sponsoring a project would have had to convince some legislative body of its merits in order to get it authorized and to get funds appropriated for it. And private sponsors would undertake only projects they considered worth while.

There would doubtless be a problem of scheduling project activations. Very likely it would not be possible to schedule activations so as to provide a perfectly timed countercycle for every business cycle. But a substantial improvement over the timing that has hitherto prevailed should surely be possible.

There would also be a financing problem. Any countercyclical expenditure program involves one, but this is not a matter that seems to call for special discussion either in connection with the buffer stock proposal or the shelf-projects proposal. In both cases I assume some form of deficit financing—that is, deficit financing during a part of each business cycle—would be called for.

The most difficult problems connected with the proposal for such a shelf seem to me to be those of providing each quarter for an adequate number of project-sponsor applications. One of these problems is certainly formidable, because to make it possible to include all the state and local government projects it might be desirable to include, extensive legal changes would be required. There would be need not only for statutory actions at all levels of government, but also for changes in municipal charters and even in state constitutions, for many state constitutions at present somewhat narrowly limit the powers of state and local governments to contract debts. During an initial period, therefore, the shelf would be restricted to projects that did not require all these legal changes.

I shall comment on only one kind of legal change that would be required for government projects, a change in appropriation procedures. At present the general rule is that an appropriation authorizes the government agency to which the appropriation is made to incur obligations, and that if any part of this authority to obligate funds is not used during the fiscal year for which the appropriation is made, that part of the authorization lapses at the end of the year, This general rule is one of the reasons why the shelf idea is difficult to work out. To meet the difficulty a special form of appropriation seems needed, a form that would provide for incurring obligations during whatever fiscal years the preparation for and operation of the project would require and that would defer the availability of most of the funds for the project's payrolls until the project had been activated.

To assure the addition to the shelf of a sufficient number of new projects each quarter, I propose that the Shelf Projects Administration should have a businesslike sales organization to sell the project agreements. This organization should be headed by a top-flight business executive who would see that the potential market was carefully analyzed so that the shelf would include the greatest possible variety of projects, and who would have a suitable form of agreement devised for each kind of project. Of course the organization would include salesmen to sell the project agreements. With an adequate sales organization enough new projects should be added to the shelf each quarter so that it would always be well stocked.

PART III. ONE WAY TO MODERATE THE WIDE CYCLICAL
FLUCTUATIONS IN PRIVATE DEMAND

The business cycle, at least in peacetime, is very largely due to the
way private construction activity and the purchases of producers' and
consumers' durable goods have been bunched in periods of active
business. The third part of the full-employment program I want to
propose for your consideration is aimed at reducing or smoothing out
this bunching.

One way to do this would use the kind of tax device, recommended
by President Kennedy, that was incorporated in the 1962 Revenue
Act, a tax credit for certain expenditures. But it would apply to the
whole area of volatile private demand, to consumers' durables and
new construction as well as to producers' durables. And it would be
a flexible or adjustable element in our tax system, not an unadjust-
able one, that is it would apply during the part of each business cycle
when there is the main need to encourage such expenditures; it
would not apply the rest of the time. Indeed if we want to move
effectively to reduce the cyclical bunching of expenditures on durable goods and new private construction, we should tax these expenditures during the periods of most active business, offer tax credits
when business is particularly slack, and have neither taxes nor credits
the rest of the time.

This kind of tax flexibility is impossible under our present procedures for levying taxes. The essence of the proposal for countercyclical variations in our incentive-tax structure is that the variations must
be made promptly to deal with each phase of the cycle as it occurs.
The legislative process is much too slow for that. It has been suggested that, to provide the kind of tax flexibility the proposal calls for,
the Congress might pass a tax law that would impose a tax on expenditures for construction and durable goods under one set of conditions and grant a tax credit under another set of conditions.
Congress could describe in general terms the conditions under which
the tax would apply, and authorize and direct some executive agency
to determine when these conditions exist and when they do not exist.
A similar procedure could be followed with the conditions for the applicability of the tax credit.

This procedure for varying countercyclically the tax incentives that
bear on the most variable private components of aggregate demand

has been criticized on the ground that it involves giving an executive agency too much discretion over taxes. There are two possible alternative procedures I will only pause to mention. One of them requires that the tax law be very specific about the applicability conditions both for the tax and for the tax credit. It would reduce the discretion exercised by the executive to a mere finding of fact. The other alternative involves a different approach to the problem of reducing the cyclical fluctuations in private construction and durable goods purchases. It is an approach I suggested in the journal article in which my proposal for a works-projects shelf was originally advanced.[5] It largely avoids the problem of giving tax discretion to an executive agency, because it depends primarily on the use of the Shelf Projects Administration's sales organization rather than on tax flexibility.

I would have liked to discuss both of these alternative procedures, had time permitted. But our present concern is to outline a program that will adequately implement the full-employment objective. I think the executive discretion procedure for varying the tax incentives that bear on private construction and durable goods purchases would clearly constitute an effective part of such a program. Indeed a small tax on these outlays during periods of particularly active business, and a small tax credit when business is especially slack, should suffice to eliminate a large part of their cyclical pattern. Our credit system would help to make this so. The announcement of the imposition of the tax during the latter part of a cyclical upswing would almost certainly cause lenders to be more cautious, and so cause a tightening of credit. Thus a credit restraint on expenditures for construction and durable goods would automatically be added to the tax.

Part III of the full-employment program I offer, then, is a counter-cyclical variation in the tax incentives that bear on the timing of most of the deferrable private expenditures on our national product so as to eliminate a large part of the bunching of these expenditures during the periods of most active business. It would change the timing, but otherwise on the average over a period of several years it would leave the composition of our national product to be determined, as it is today, by supply-and-demand adjustments. It would operate within our free enterprise system and have its impact on the level and timing

[5] Copeland, "Business Stabilization by Agreement," pp. 328–339.

of aggregate demand; the price and cost factors that determine the apportionment of our resources now would continue to operate much as they have been operating heretofore.

On the whole the same can be said of Parts I and II of the program I have offered. The buffer stock operation I have suggested is a proposal for price stabilization—taking most of the cycle out of the prices of a number of staple commodities. It is not a valorization proposal. And my suggestion for implementing the idea of a works-projects shelf is concerned with the control of the timing of the shelf projects, not with the merits of the projects or with their average annual dollar volume. I think it would be unwise to have the Shelf Projects Administration at all concerned with their merits. As at present, a government agency sponsoring a project would have to convince the Congress, or the state or local legislature concerned, to authorize it and to appropriate money for it. It is true the selling activities of the Shelf Projects Administration plus the bonus it would offer for shelf projects might slightly increase the quinquennial average dollar volume of government GNP expenditures. But the increase would be very small, and there is no reason to think boondoggling projects would be significantly encouraged.

PART IV. A CONSUMER-INCOME SUBSIDY

All three of the proposals I have thus far made seem to assume that, if we can somehow iron out the business cycle, we shall have solved the problem of full employment. But the problem is not only one of the business cycle; there is also the possibility of a secular deficiency in aggregate demand.

I have purposely confined the objective that would be served by the first three parts of the program I am proposing to that of ironing out the cycle. The remaining part is particularly designed to deal with a secular deficiency in aggregate demand.

Let us assume at this point that Parts I, II, and III of my proposed program are in operation, and that together they have the effect of eliminating nearly all of the cyclical variation in the dollar amount of GNP. Let us assume, too, that the GNP each quarter is somewhat below a full-employment level, and that the approximate dollar amount that we would need to add to aggregate demand each quarter to provide full employment has been determined. It will be convenient to call this amount Delta GNP. Conceivably Delta GNP could be added to any of the main components of the national product. However, there is reason to rule out the export surplus, both because it is so small and because of the international complications any attempt to increase it would entail. There is reason, too, to hold that the main increase should not be concentrated in private-capital formation. As a long-run adjustment a given increase in personal consumption expenditure plus government GNP expenditure would call for a so-called "derived demand" addition to private capital formation; there is a balance between private capital formation and the rest of aggregate demand that should be maintained in planning the Delta GNP.

The proposal I want to submit for your consideration assumes that measures should be taken to add enough to personal consumption expenditure, say X dollars, so that X dollars plus the addition that these dollars would call for in private capital formation would be equal to Delta GNP. This means that the measures to make up the secular deficiency in aggregate demand would focus on personal consumption expenditure, that there would be no attempt to make up any part of this deficiency by developing additional government expenditure programs.

There would be serious administrative difficulties in developing additional government expenditure programs to increase total GNP. Such expenditure programs should certainly meet three requirements. First, they should be genuinely worth while, more worth while than possible alternatives. Second, they should not compete with actual or potential private undertakings. And third, they should avoid anything savoring of a pork-barrel operation. It is unlikely that all three of these requirements could be met. If it were decided to develop additional government expenditure programs to increase GNP, I think it is safe to predict that the result would be either substantial competition with private undertakings or a pork-barrel operation that involved extensive boondoggling.

Measures to increase personal consumption expenditures are to be preferred to attempts to develop additional government expenditure programs partly because of these administrative considerations. But a more telling consideration is that such measures can mean increases in personal freedom, while adding to government expenditure programs in general would not. The measures to increase personal consumption expenditures I propose would provide money to finance them and leave consumers free to decide how to spend the money. Twenty odd years ago John Pierson made a proposal along these lines, and Part IV of the program I offer is essentially his proposal.[6]

As Pierson made clear, there are various consumption financing measures that would leave the consumer free to decide what he wants to buy. One way that Pierson considered would be to cut taxes. Another would be to subsidize consumer incomes. Pierson suggested the possibility of a subsidy of so much per capita per quarter to everybody, the size of the per capita payment for each quarter being determined on the basis of the level of GNP and of employment in the immediately preceding period. Such a subsidy would have the advantage over an individual income-tax cut that the addition to GNP per dollar of cost to the government would probably be appreciably larger. This is so because some of the subsidy would go to persons in the lowest income brackets and because the marginal propensity to consume is presumably higher for such persons than it is for those who pay income taxes. Besides this advantage there is the theoretical possibility that a larger stimulus might be needed than a tax cut to zero could provide. But this possibility is probably so remote that we can disregard it. In any event, we do not need to decide here between the tax-cut method of stimulating an increase in aggregate demand and the income subsidy. It should be possible by either method to provide a sufficient stimulus.

If we had the three anticyclical parts of our hypothetical full-employment program in operation, we cannot be certain that there would still be a problem of a secular deficiency in aggregate demand. Today it seems probable that there would be. But for completeness we should recognize that a secular surplus of aggregate demand is certainly conceivable. For such a situation, if there were to be one, Pierson suggested a broad consumption-expenditure tax. But perhaps it should be an ad valorem surtax added to the individual income tax.

Clearly a steering-wheel policy requires restraints on aggregate demand as well as stimuli. If we succeeded in keeping the economy operating at substantially a full-employment level for any considerable period of time, the gradual upward movement of prices we have had during recent years would doubtless be appreciably accelerated. And to avoid the sharper price increases excessive demand pressures would involve, it would be urgent to have prompt means of restricting demand. Perhaps the means provided by Parts I, II, and III of our

[6] John H. G. Pierson, "The Underwriting of Consumer Spending as a Pillar of Full Employment Policy," *American Economic Review*, XXXIV (March 1944), 21–55.

program would suffice. But it would be well also to have a broad consumption tax or else an income surtax that could, if need be, be resorted to as a further restraint.

We have been considering the problem that would remain, if Parts I, II, and III of our full employment program were in operation. My proposal for dealing with a secular deficiency in aggregate demand, if there were one, is to increase disposable consumer income. I think the simplest way to do this is through a consumer-income subsidy. What this would mean financially for the federal government would depend on the situation before the subsidy went into effect. Let us suppose that in this previous situation what are called federal government receipts from the public were just equal to federal government payments to the public. In other words let us suppose in this hypothetical situation that the government cash budget was in balance. Then the subsidy would presumably mean, for each quarter to which it applied, a federal cash deficit. I think I have shown how we could effectively implement the full-employment objective, how we could make the fiscal policy changes each quarter that a steering-wheel approach would require. The measures I have proposed would, if there proved to be a secular deficiency in aggregate demand, probably involve deficit financing. I have not tried to consider whether there would be any way to avoid deficit financing.

Some twenty years ago Lord Beveridge in his *Full Employment in a Free Society* presented his ideas on how to implement a full employment program.[7] He proposed several alternative procedures; he called them alternative "routes to full employment." He assumed, as did Nicholas Kaldor who collaborated with him, that it would be possible to have an additional government expenditure bring about an increase in aggregate demand, even though it was fully financed by added taxes. One of his proposed routes to full employment involved no deficit financing. The question whether a secular deficiency in aggregate demand could be made up without government deficit financing is a complicated one, and one that has not been very fully explored. I shall not try to go into it here. Beveridge and Kaldor may well have been right in assuming the answer is Yes. At all events, if we decide to implement the full employment objective, as I think we should, investigating this question should be an early order of business.

[7] William H. Beveridge, *Full Employment in a Free Society* (New York: Norton, 1944).

Concluding Comments

The program I offer, then consists of these four parts: Part I, The buffer stock operation; Part II, The works-projects shelf; Part III, Countercyclical variations in the tax incentives that bear on private construction and durable goods purchases; and Part IV, The consumer-income subsidy.

The program I have offered may, by some, be considered a radical one. It is radical in the sense that it is markedly different from the policy we have been following. It needs to be. We cannot expect to achieve the full-employment objective at any calculable date with the easy-going, half-hearted policy that has characterized government actions during the past twenty years. The measures adopted must be adequate, to promise reasonably prompt results. I think the measures I propose are adequate.

I said in the beginning that I would not argue the case for implementing the full-employment objective. I have not been concerned to consider what our government's policy ought to be. I have attempted to show, and I believe I have shown, by the program I have proposed that we can adequately implement the full-employment objective, if that is what we want to do.

In an important sense the program I have offered is a conservative one. It has been specifically drawn to conserve our personal freedom and our free enterprise type of economy. It would strengthen the role of consumers' freedom of choice in determining the composition of our national product. The fluctuations in that product would be smoothed out, and its level would be higher, but the profit system and market adjustments would continue to play the same dominant parts in organizing economic activity that they have been playing, and they would continue to govern the apportionment of our resources.

Let me add just one more comment. Some may object to my program because in at least one respect it does not go far enough, because the problem of inadequate aggregate demand is more than a national problem, is in fact a problem for the whole free world. Admittedly it is. And admittedly only Part I of the program I have offered is international in scope. But that is the part it is urgent to have international. That is the part concerned with stabilizing the incomes of the raw material producing countries that have been so sensitive to cyclical fluctuations in world aggregate demand. As for the other three parts of the program, first, I think it is clear that the United States, as the principal industrialized nation of the free world, is in a position to operate these parts of the program all by itself. And second, since this country has come to be known and to be feared as the chief exporter of business depressions, I think we have an obligation to become a good economic neighbor, an obligation to smooth out the cycle in our demands for the goods that other countries produce.

GARDINER C. MEANS

Monetary Institutions
to Serve the Modern Economy

IF A MAN FROM MARS came to study the economy of our country, he could be expected to reach some very strange conclusions about our monetary institutions.

First, he would discover that money is at the heart of our free enterprise system. Indeed, he might justifiably conclude that money provides the powerhouse that makes the economy run.

Second, he would discover that our monetary institutions are so complex that relatively few people, outside of the specialists in the field, understand how money is created or how its supply can be reduced. Few intelligent laymen could tell him what constitutes money or how changes in the money supply are brought about. He would find it strange that so few engineers, or lawyers or business-men or public administrators or congressmen know the answers.

Third, he would be surprised at how little agreement there is even among the specialists on how this powerhouse works or how its working affects the operation of the economy. The experts are not even agreed on what constitutes money. They are not agreed on how changes in the money supply affect the demand for goods. And we currently have some monetary experts advocating a reduction in the money supply in order to improve the operation of the econ-omy while other monetary experts are advocating an increase for the same purpose.

We can see the man from Mars returning to his planet shaking his head at his strange experience with a society which relies on money as a basic institution in the operation of its economy and yet so clearly knows so little about how that institution actually works.

In this paper I shall present my views on this basic institution. In particular I am going to set forth what I believe to be the most important function of monetary policy under modern conditions and the institutional changes which are needed in order that this function should be performed well.

I plan to break my discussion into two separate sections. The first will be primarily a theoretical discussion of the effects of monetary change as it influences employment and the function of monetary policy in supporting aggregate demand. The second section will be concerned with our actual monetary institutions and ways in which they could be modified so that the essential function I outline could be better performed.

Theories of Money and Employment

Now for theory. It is quite generally accepted that monetary policy must be concerned with economic stability. For most specialists this also means that it must be concerned with the employment of men and machines and the demand which stimulates such employment. But the specialists differ on how monetary policy affects demand and how demand affects employment. It will help to clarify these relations if we first examine two theories of employment, the classical and the Keynesian, and show why neither is appropriate to the modern problem.

THE CLASSICAL THEORY OF EMPLOYMENT

It is often said that the classical economists had no theory of employment, or that they *assumed* full employment. Thus Keynes says at the outset of his general theory, "The classical postulates do not admit of the possibility of ... involuntary unemployment."[1]

But a careful examination of the classical writers does disclose a theory of employment which postulates involuntary unemployment and provides a mechanism which would tend automatically to eliminate it.[2] This mechanism is not clearly articulated but it so obviously

[1] J. M. Keynes, *The General Theory of Employment, Interest and Money* (New York: Macmillan, 1936), p. 6.

[2] Keynes includes as "classical" writers not only Ricardo and James Mill but also J. S. Mill, Marshall, Edgeworth, and Pigou (*Ibid.*, p. 3). It is clear that

underlies the classical discussions of money and so closely parallels the Ricardian theory of international trade adjustment that I think we can take it as given.

This classical theory of employment adjustment can be outlined in six simple steps.

1. Assume an initial condition in which there is extensive involuntary unemployment, a fixed money supply, and perfectly flexible prices and wage rates.

2. Competition among workers for jobs and among producers to sell their products would force down both wage rates and prices but this would not, in itself, increase employment because money incomes would necessarily go down along with lower prices and wages.

3. With the nominal money supply constant, the fall in the price-wage level would so increase the real value of money that money would become redundant—Ricardo's term for money in excess of the amount the public would choose to hold at the current level of real incomes and prices.

4. The public, finding a part of its money holdings redundant, would seek to dispose of the excess through buying goods, thus creating demand in excess of that arising from the spending of current incomes.

5. This purchase of extra goods would create additional income and employment and the redundancy of money would be reduced as the increase in real incomes increased the real buying power the public would choose to hold in the form of money.

Marshall's *Principles* does assume full employment. It is concerned *solely* with the mechanisms which direct resources into different uses under conditions of full employment and a practically stable price level. But Marshall made clear in his prefaces, particularly in the preface to his second edition, that the microeconomic analysis of his *Principles* was to be followed by one or two other volumes which would deal with money and what we now call involuntary unemployment.

It may well be that Pigou, on whom Keynes relies for his statement of the classical position on employment (*Ibid.*, pp. 5–7 and Appendix to Chapter 19), did, in effect, assume full employment as Keynes says and did not conceive of a mechanism which would tend automatically to correct involuntary unemployment. But J. S. Mill clearly did have in mind the concept of involuntary unemployment and a mechanism which tended to eliminate it automatically as indicated in the text below. For Mill, full employment is not an assumption, but an equilibrium conclusion which tends to be automatically approximated through the mechanism of employment adjustment operating through changes in the price level and thereby in the real value of the money stock.

6. The fall in the price-wage level and the rise in employment would continue until all downward price-wage pressure was eliminated by the disappearance of involuntary unemployment. At this point there would cease to be any redundance in the money supply and the public would *seek* to spend on consumption and investment goods neither more nor less than the whole of its current income.

That such a theory was implicit in classical thinking is suggested by John Stuart Mill's discussion of overproduction.[3] He states that general overproduction is not theoretically possible but then goes on to suggest that in one sense, there can be *temporary* overproduction, saying "At such times there is really an excess of all commodities above the money demand: in other words there is an under-supply of money" and goes on to suggest that this would lead to "an extreme depression of general prices, from what may indiscriminately be called a glut of commodities or a dearth of money." He also indicates that, if other forces did not do so, the fall in prices would eliminate the overproduction or dearth of money and adds with respect to the fall in prices, "The fall being solely of money prices, if prices did not rise again no dealer would lose, since the smaller price would be worth as much to him as the larger price was before." Thus according to Mill overproduction could only be a temporary phenomenon.

There are two characteristics of this classical theory of employment adjustment which should be noticed. First it depended on the short-run flexibility of prices and wage rates. Later we will come back to this assumption which is so much in conflict with the realities of our modern economy. And second it assumes that money has a direct effect on demand.

It is this second assumption, implicit in the concept of redundant money, which deserves our immediate attention. The redundancy of money means that, at the current level of real incomes and prices, the public has more money on hand than it chooses to hold. And, as we all know too well, if you have more cash on hand than you choose to hold, it is very easy to get rid of the extra by spending it. This conception of the direct effect of money on aggregate demand runs through the whole of the classical discussions of money and of international theory and provides a logical justification for Say's law. This direct effect is presumed to operate whether the real money

[3] John Stuart Mill, *Principles of Political Economy* (London: Longmans, Green, 1926), pp. 557–561.

supply is increased by a fall in the price level or by an increase in the stock of money. It provides classical theory with a cybernetic mechanism which automatically tends to maintain full employment. According to this theory, if prices and wage rates were perfectly flexible, involuntary unemployment could not survive the automatic forces of supply and demand.

KEYNES' THEORY OF EMPLOYMENT

Keynes provides us with quite a different theory of employment. Neglecting the classical assumption of the direct effect of money on demand, or perhaps unaware of it, he built his theory on what we can call the interest effect of money on demand. Keynes assumed that the *only* way a change in the real supply of money can influence aggregate demand is through interest rates. An increase in the real money supply can reduce interest rates, this stimulates investment and the extra investment puts to work the extra savings which would occur at a higher level of income, thereby increasing aggregate demand. Similarly, a contraction in the real money supply would raise interest rates and reduce aggregate demand.

The aim of Keynes' theory was to explain persistent involuntary unemployment even under conditions of perfectly flexible prices and wage rates.[4] And it is important for us to recognize that, *if we accept his basic monetary assumption,* his theory would provide such an explanation. If the only way an increase in the real money supply could affect aggregate demand were through interest rates, involuntary unemployment which caused a fall in the price-wage level could increase aggregate demand by increasing the real value of the money supply, thereby reducing interest rates and stimulating investment. But then some minimum level of interest rates would be reached

---

[4] It is well recognized that two employment theories can be derived from Keynes' *General Theory,* one based on liquidity preference and one on wage inflexibility. When I first read the *General Theory* I was aware that its explanation of persistent unemployment could rest on wage inflexibility and therefore be a variant of the explanation I had already made public in 1935 (*Industrial Prices and Their Relative Inflexibility,* Document No. 13, 74th Congress, 1st Session [Washington, D.C.: U.S. Government Printing Office, 1935]) or it could rest on liquidity preference. For this reason I visited Keynes at his country place in Sussex in the summer of 1939 in order to discover to what extent his theory rested on the inflexibility of wage rates. His answer was clear and unequivocal. He said that, if prices and wage rates were perfectly flexible so that the real value of the money supply could be increased indefinitely, this could not reduce involuntary unemployment except as it was able to reduce interest rates.

(Keynes suggested 2 per cent) below which rates could not be pushed and any further increase in the real value of the money supply would have *no* significant effect on aggregate demand. This is Keynes' famous liquidity trap. In the Keynesian model, even with perfectly flexible prices and wage rates, involuntary unemployment could persist with no automatic corrective in the system.

It is also part of the Keynesian theory that even before the liquidity trap is reached, the stimulating effect of lower interest rates on aggregate demand is of secondary importance. The purchase of investment goods is not greatly altered by 1 or 2 per cent change in interest rates. It is for this reason that the followers of Keynes place primary emphasis on fiscal policy and minimize the importance of monetary policy. These are reasonable conclusions if we accept Keynes' assumption that the only way money can affect aggregate demand is through interest rates.

Here we have two quite different ideas as to the effect of money on aggregate demand. Does money affect demand directly as the classical theory implies or does it operate only through interest rates as Keynes assumes? This is a crucial question which must be answered before we can discuss our monetary institutions intelligently.

THE DIRECT EFFECT OF MONEY ON DEMAND

Nowhere in his *General Theory* does Keynes discuss the direct effect of money on spending. Indeed he seems to be unaware of the classical assumption. As a result, he has given us no reasoned explanation of why we should reject that assumption.

Yet it must be clear that, at least in some circumstances, money must have a direct effect on demand. Consider, for example, an economic model in which goods and labor are bought and sold for money but in which there are *no credit transactions*. Then interest rates on loans could not play a role. Any redundancy of money must operate directly on aggregate demand by increasing the propensity to consume or the propensity to invest or both. The only way an individual could dispose of extra money would be to buy goods or labor. He would then be spending more on consumption and investment goods than he received as income and would be creating additional income for someone else. If the money supply was fixed, the society as a whole could not dispose of redundant money. Only as its aggregate demand increased would money cease to be redundant. Thus in a model without credit, money must have a direct effect on aggregate demand. For such a model the classical assumption would seem to be valid.

If we introduce credit into the model, we provide individuals with an alternative between holding money and lending it as well as that between holding and spending. And there is ample evidence that the amount of money people choose to hold is influenced by interest rates as Keynes suggests. I think we must accept Keynes' theory of liquidity preference and his liquidity trap. But does this mean that we must at the same time reject the classical assumption of a direct effect? Can money affect demand in only one way? Or can there be both an interest effect and a direct effect?

The issue can be brought to a focus by examining Keynes' liquidity trap. As the trap level of interest rates is reached, according to Keynes, any stimulus to demand and employment from an increase in the real money supply would disappear. At that low level of interest rates, any further addition to the real money supply, whether through a fall in the price-wage level or through monetary expansion, would have no significant effect on interest rates and therefore no significant effect on aggregate demand. At this level, according to Keynes, the public would choose to hold any amount of money rather than do something with it.

It is this last conclusion which is at issue. One can agree with Keynes that some level of interest rates will be so low that the public would choose to hold any amount of money *rather than make additional loans*. But would the public hold any amount of money *rather than spend more on goods?*

Let us take an extreme example. Suppose that involuntary unemployment developed in an economy with perfectly flexible prices and wage rates and with a fixed money supply. Also assume that a fall in the price-wage level has already so increased the real money supply that the liquidity trap has been reached so that no further increase in the money supply can bring a significant further reduction in interest rates. At this point, according to Keynes, any further increase in the money supply would cease to have any significant effect on aggregate demand.

But consider the effect of a further fall in the price-wage level. Assume that when the trap level of interest rates were reached, the public had the equivalent of a quarter of a year's real income in the form of money on hand. As the price-wage level fell, the real value of the public's money holdings would increase. If the price level dropped to 1 per cent of its initial level, the public would be holding the equivalent of twenty-five years of annual income in the form of money. At this point, Keynes would have to say that, since the liquidity trap had already been reached, the public would choose to hold the whole of the increase in the real supply of money and not spend any of it on buying more goods, no matter how large the real buying power of the fixed money supply might become. It is because Keynes never posed the question in these terms that the absurdity of his assumption escaped him. Certainly, long before the public held the equivalent of twenty-five years worth of real income in the form of cash balances, the money supply would become redundant in relation to goods and extra spending would take place. Thus the direct effect of money on demand would operate even though interest rates had fallen to the level of the liquidity trap. And this effect alone would be sufficient to restore full employment in the flexible-priced model posited both by the classical writers and by Keynes.

This conclusion destroys the effectiveness of Keynes' theory as an explanation of persistent unemployment. The classical theory can be modified to take account of Keynes' liquidity preference and still reach the conclusion that, in a flexible-price economy, there is an automatic mechanism which will tend to eliminate involuntary unemployment. But Keynes' theory of employment cannot be modified to take account of the direct effect of money on demand without destroying its ability to explain persistent unemployment in an economy of perfectly flexible prices and wage rates. If one accepts the direct effect of money on demand, and there is considerable empirical evidence in support, then one must conclude that Say's law would operate in a perfectly flexible-priced economy even when Keynes' liquidity preference and liquidity trap are introduced. Keynes made an important contribution when he introduced these concepts but he did not explain equilibrium at less than full employment.

THE INFLEXIBILITY OF PRICES AND WAGE RATES

To explain persistent unemployment, I believe we must turn to the other major element in the classical employment theory, the assumption of short-run flexibility of prices and wage rates. Our man from Mars would quickly spot the fact that the great bulk of our prices are administered and tend to be inflexible in the short run while wage rates tend to be set for a year or more at a time. Prices and wage rates today simply do not have the short-run flexibility that is assumed in classical theory. If involuntary unemployment developed with a fixed money supply and a fixed price and wage level, there would be no automatic corrective for unemployment. And, if prices and wage rates were not fixed but were relatively inflexible, the classical corrective mechanism could be so slow as to create persistent unemployment while the price and wage distortions which would result between the more and the less flexible would not be socially acceptable, as we found in the 1930's.

On the basis of this analysis and my studies of price behavior, I have reached two basic conclusions. *First, that persistant unemployment is not a product of liquidity preference but of price and wage inflexibility. And second, that in our modern economy, prices and wages cannot be made sufficiently flexible to allow the classical employment-adjustment mechanism to work.*

This leads to the same general policy conclusion reached by Keynes that we must find measures to support aggregate demand to the extent required for full employment at a relatively stable price level. But this conclusion is reached on quite different grounds and with quite different implications for specific policy. Keynes' conclusion does not rest at all on the assumption of price and wage inflexibility but rests on the assumption that money affects aggregate demand only through interest rates. My own policy conclusion rests wholly on the inflexibility of prices and wages and is not in conflict with the classical assumption that money has a direct effect on demand. If money affects aggregate demand only through interest rates and if liquidity preference is the essential source of general unemployment, then one must agree with the Keynesian view that monetary measures provide only a weak instrument for establishing the necessary aggregate demand; if money has a direct effect on demand and the inflexibility of prices and wage rates is the source, then monetary measures provide a powerful instrument for establishing the demand necessary for full employment. Both theories suggest that fiscal policy can be used as an instrument for influencing demand, but the Keynesian theory makes it the major instrument while the alternative theory makes money the major instrument. Indeed, if we accept the conclusion that money has a direct effect on demand, then monetary policy can be used to provide the appropriate amount of aggregate demand whether the federal budget is in balance, in surplus, or in deficit though of course the monetary action would be different in the three situations.

THE BASIC FULL-EMPLOYMENT POLICY

This leads me to my most basic policy recommendation: *That it be the prime function of monetary policy to provide that volume of money and only that volume which the public would choose to hold at full employment and the prevailing price and wage levels.*

You will notice that in this statement of function, I say nothing about inflation or the balance of external payments.

With respect to inflation, I distinguish between two kinds, demand inflation and administrative inflation, or what is sometimes misleadingly called cost-push inflation. The first comes from excessive aggregate demand and it should be the responsibility of monetary policy to prevent demand inflation. But this responsibility is indicated in the policy as I have stated it. Demand inflation would arise only if the monetary authorities created *more* money than the public would choose to hold at full employment and the prevailing price and wage level and this would be in conflict with the recommended policy.

On the other hand, I do not think that monetary policy should be used to inhibit administrative inflation. It is quite possible that a monetary policy which maintained employment well below the level of full employment could reduce the pressures which lead to administrative inflation though the fact that the steel industry was operating at way below its capacity did not prevent it from generating administrative inflation in the mid-1950's. But the use of monetary policy to control administrative inflation by creating unemployment is equivalent to saying, we will let the weakest part of our society bear the burden of preventing administrative inflation because we are unwilling to take the necessary nonmonetary measures. I believe that nonmonetary measures can be effectively used to prevent administrative inflation without interfering with the operation of our free enterprise system. But that is another story.

I reach a similar conclusion with respect to the balance of external payments. I do not think that the money supply should be kept at a level below that needed for full employment in order to minimize an unbalance in external payments. To do so would again be to place the burden of adjustment on the unemployed in order to avoid taking the appropriate nonmonetary measures or monetary measures within the framework of full employment. I believe a set of policies can be worked out to maintain an acceptable balance of external payments without using unemployment as an instrument. But again, that is another story.

So I will conclude this theoretical section of my paper by taking the anti-Keynesian position that monetary policy can be a powerful instrument for maintaining that level of aggregate demand necessary for full employment, and I suggest that it should be the primary instrument to that end.

Changes in Our Monetary Institutions

Now let me turn to the institutional changes which could make our monetary policy more effective in maintaining full employment and preventing demand inflation. I will take up these changes under three headings. The first group of changes would be those which could be made without any new legislation. I believe there is much room for improvement without Congressional action. The second group of institutional changes would call for Congressional action, but only action of a very mild character. The third group of institutional changes would require more fundamental legislation but could yield what I would regard as an ideal set of monetary institutions capable of providing the most constructive instrument for monetary policy.

All of the institutional changes I will suggest are aimed at increasing the ability of our monetary authority, the Board of Governors of the Federal Reserve System, to control the outstanding money supply *so that it is just, and only just, equal to the amount of money the public would choose to hold at full employment and the prevailing price level.* I do not want to suggest that this aim can be perfectly fulfilled. But I do suggest that it is the only realistic goal of monetary policy and that we can organize our monetary institutions to achieve the essentials of this goal.

Institutional Changes without Legislation

As I see it, there are three important institutional changes which could be made without legislation and which would allow great improvement in monetary policy. The power to make these changes already rests with the Federal Reserve Board.

The first is a shift in orientation from a focus on credit to a focus on the creating of money and particularly on the amount of money the public would choose to hold at different levels of economic activity.

When the Federal Reserve System was created back in 1913 it was focused on commercial credit and not on maintaining the appropriate supply of money. This was, in part, a reaction to the gold panic of 1907 when the credit system broke down so completely that credit was not available even for legitimate and thoroughly responsible borrowers. In those circumstances it is not surprising that the only specific purposes stated in the preamble of the Federal Reserve Act, apart from the creation of the Federal Reserve banks and the regulation of banks, are "to furnish an elastic currency," and "to afford means of rediscounting commercial paper." The first of these purposes was concerned with currency which represents only a small part of our actual money supply and the second was focused on the needs of business for commercial credit and not with the needs of the economy for an adequate but not excessive supply of money.

Only gradually has it come to be recognized that Federal Reserve policy in large measure determines the volume of the money supply and that this, rather than the supplying of business credit, is the primary function of the Federal Reserve System. The credit orientation has so dominated the thinking about the System that it was not until 1960 that the *Federal Reserve Bulletin* devoted a Table to "Money Supply" in its monthly compilation of financial and business statistics. During the first thirty years in the life of the System, one had to discover the amount of the money supply by combining the separate figures on currency and on deposits and these were in two different parts of the *Federal Reserve Bulletin*.

Furthermore, while the *Bulletin* provides us with detailed monthly figures on credit—how much each category of banks has loaned and how much has been borrowed by different types of borrowers—until recently we were provided with almost nothing on who holds the outstanding money supply—how much is held by business, how much by government institutions, and how much by consumers.

Even more curious, monetary policy is discussed primarily in terms of credit. Thus, the Federal Reserve Board report on Bank Credit and Monetary Developments for the year 1964 (*Federal Reserve Bulletin,* February 1965) presents on its first page a chart on "Bank Credit" but not until its seventh page are we given a chart on the "Money

Supply" while the thirteen-page report is mostly devoted to bank credit and gives only three paragraphs to the money supply.

The same attitude is reflected in public discussions of monetary policy. The current policy is discussed in terms of a tight or an easy credit policy, not in terms of monetary expansion or contraction.

Not until Federal Reserve Policy is clearly focused on the country's needs for a money supply can we expect effective policy to result. Such an institutional shift would assume that the amount of bank credit which the banking system could properly create through creating money would be determined entirely by how much money the public would choose to hold at full employment, not by the amount of credit business or others might seek. And the level of interest rates would be determined by the relation between the demand for investment funds and the community's saving, including both the amount that the community would choose to save by adding to its money holdings and the amount it would choose to save in other forms. As Keynes has properly pointed out, saving and investment as currently defined are in the final analysis only opposite aspects of the same thing. Also, as Keynes has shown, interest rates influence the quantity of money which the public chooses to hold. This means that saving and investment, interest rates and money are all interrelated like three balls in a bowl. Change any one, and the other two are bound to adjust. It follows that the institutional shift required is one which shifts the focus from the saving-investment-credit and the interest-rate balls to the money ball. The basic problem of monetary policy is then to manipulate the money ball into the position at which the money supply is just right for full employment while the supply of credit and the level of interest rates are a derived result, not the focus, of policy.

I do not want to suggest that such a policy would be easy to follow. There is first the question of what constitutes full employment. This is in part a question of social policy. The present Administration has suggested that the employment of 97 per cent of the labor force as now measured would constitute full employment. I believe the Federal Reserve Board should adopt as its policy aim whatever figure for full employment is adopted by the then prevailing Administration unless there were profound reasons for rejecting it.

More difficult is the problem of estimating how much money the public would choose to hold at full employment. This should be the most important function of the Federal Reserve Board. It requires an estimate by the Board not of how much money the public will choose to hold in the immediate future but how much it is likely to want to hold in the near future *at full employment.*

Certain aspects of such a forecast would not be difficult. The Board now as a matter of routine makes estimates of seasonal fluctuations in the public's demand for cash balances and *as a matter of institutional policy* it adjusts the money supply up or down to take account of them. Thus it meets the pre-Christmas increase in the public's desire for cash balances and the post-Christmas decline. Similarly it meets the greater requirements for cash balances at harvest time. These are routine.

Some other shifts in the demand for money at full employment could be forecast without too great acumen. The outbreak of a major war would usually be a signal for a decline in the demand for cash balances as housewives can be expected to shift from money into groceries likely to be rationed and business executives shift from money into inventories likely to be scarce. Such forecasts would indicate the need for some contraction or slowing up in the expansion of the money supply.

But the month-to-month adjustments in the money supply would have to be made on the basis of more complex forecasts.

One procedure that has been suggested is a standard annual increase in the money supply at a specified rate, presumably combined with seasonal variation. But to forecast that the public will choose to increase its money holdings at full employment at any specified rate from year to year seems to me to deny the complexity of human behavior. There is much evidence that changes in short-term interest rates affect the amount of money the public chooses to hold. And statistical analysis suggests that other factors than interest rates and the size of the public's real income affect the real balances the public chooses to hold. It seems to me almost certain that a rigid annual rate of growth in the money supply would lead to significant and harmful fluctuations in aggregate demand.

Another procedure is to assume that whenever employment is below the full-employment level, there is a deficiency in the money supply and whenever it is above there is a surplus. This procedure has the appearance of avoiding the need for forecasting but actually it makes the forecast that in the short run the propensity to hold money will remain constant, which is almost as bad as forecasting

that it will increase at a standard rate. And besides, on the down-
side it would place a burden of unemployment on workers in order
to provide a signal and on the up side would require conditions of
demand inflation to provide a signal. Of course, when employment
was substantially below full employment—as at present—this would
signal the need for expansion in the money supply. Likewise, if there
were clear evidence of demand inflation, this would signal the need
for a limitation on the supply. But to wait for such signals is to create
unnecessary hardships.

The more appropriate procedure would seem to me to be continuous forecasting of the public's demand for cash balances at full employment. This would be done on the basis of long-run trends, short-
run seasonal factors, the closeness to the aim of full employment, and
a comprehensive analysis of the actual factors which lead individuals
and business enterprises to change the amounts of money they choose
to hold. Careful analysis of the quarterly data on money flows which
is now available over a considerable period should throw light on
such factors. And I believe the forecasting could be developed to
the point where it could be a reasonably reliable guide to policy.
Certainly it would not be perfect but, used with judgment, it could
be very much superior to any procedures now used for determining
monetary policy. It could also be superior to a fixed rate of growth or
to reliance on the twin signals of excessive unemployment and demand inflation.

Once we have made this institutional change from focusing Federal Reserve policy on credit to focusing it on the money supply, we
can expect the first chart in the Federal Reserve Board's annual report
on Monetary Policy to be a chart on the money supply. Likewise, the
first chart in the Board's Chart Book would be one showing changes
in the total money supply outstanding followed by charts showing
changes in the amounts of money held by different types of institutions and individuals. And an effective policy would so adjust the
money supply as to maintain the combined propensities to consume
and invest at the levels necessary for full employment.

The second institutional change that seems to me called for has to
do with the mechanism for controlling the supply of money. I have
implied in the foregoing that the Federal Reserve Board has the
power to control the money supply. It certainly has this power and it
has consciously exercised this power. But the power has grown a
little like Topsy. It is a very loose-jointed affair with a great deal of

slack and uncertainty. In the exercise of this power the Board has adopted a set of institutional policies such that when it increases bank reserves there tends to be a drift upward in the money supply and when it reduces reserves there tends to be a downward drift. This policy is guided by the amount of net free reserves in the system, that is, reserves which could legally be the basis for bank credit expansion but are not currently being used. It is the total unused reserves in the system less the amount of borrowed reserves. This is a somewhat cumbersome way of exercising a rough and not always ready control over the money supply. It reminds me of an old style freight train before air brakes were invented. The train could be stopped but only with a great jolting and jouncing in the process. We need institutional arrangements such that the monetary authority can exercise a reasonably precise and positive control over the money supply.

To outline an alternative institution I must first draw a sharp distinction between legal reserves and economic reserves. The legal reserves are obviously the reserves that a bank is required to hold by law. But even if there were no legal requirement, banks would find it necessary to hold reserves simply to be able to stay in business. Presumably, with no legal requirement, the very conservative banks would hold large reserves against their deposit liabilities; less conservative banks would hold proportionately smaller reserves; and some reckless banks would hold quite inadequate reserves. Thus we can speak of the economic reserves as the reserves which banks would hold if there were no legal requirements.

Originally the primary function of the legal-reserve requirements was to increase the safety of the banking systems by forcing the less conservative banks to hold more reserves than they would choose to hold if left to themselves. But the fact that legal reserves tended to be above the economically necessary reserves meant that there was a quick response to any changes in the amount of reserves in the banking system. If available reserves were increased by say 1 per cent, banks would quickly increase their portfolio of loans and investments and thereby increase the money supply. Similarly, a reduction in bank reserves would quickly lead to a reduction in the money supply. Thus, under the old gold standard before the creation of the Federal Reserve System, the money supply tended to vary closely with changes in the supply of bank reserves.

But today there is more play in our system. The presence of free reserves suggests that many banks, particularly country banks with their lower-reserve requirements, want to hold more reserves than the law requires while many other banks must be close to the line where their legal reserves are not much above their economic requirements. And for still others, some of their legal reserves are obtained by borrowing from the Reserve banks so that the amount of reserves they own, net of such debt, is close to their economic requirements. Under these conditions, the response to changes in the amount of reserves created by the Federal Reserve banks tends to be slower, sometimes lagging as much as three or four months. The most that can be expected is that there will be a somewhat lagging and imprecise change in the money supply for any given change in reserves.

Two changes could be made which would greatly increase the Reserve Board's control over the money supply. The first is to raise reserve requirements on demand deposits so that, *for practically every member bank*, the legal reserve requirement is well above its economic requirement. The second is to raise the discount rate to such a level that the discount privilege is rarely used and changes in discount rate cease to be an instrument of current monetary policy. Such an institutional shift would mean that banks in their loan and investment policies would maintain a position of being "fully loaned up" without borrowing from the Reserve banks and that any change in reserves created by the Reserve banks would be quickly and precisely reflected in changes in the money supply. Also, while a bank could fall back on its Reserve bank for reserves in an emergency, it would only do so at a substantial cost. These two changes would give the Reserve Board a much more positive control over the money supply and thus help it to carry out its basic monetary responsibility.

Such a change of institutional policy should of course be realized gradually. In moving toward such a new situation, the higher reserve requirements could be a burden on individual banks. When I discuss new legislation I will outline a proposal which would largely if not wholly remove this burden. But even if the latter proposal is not adopted, the burden on individual banks would be small compared to the public benefit from more positive control over the money supply. And it would be less of a burden if the adjustment were made slowly or in conjunction with the new legislation I propose.

Such a change in institutional policy would complete the shift from policy emphasis on discount rate to open-market operations and would make open-market operations the heart of Federal Reserve

Policy. In the original development of the Reserve System, it was expected that the discount rate would be the primary instrument of policy and that bank reserves would be increased or decreased as member banks borrowed more or less from the Reserve banks, subject to partial control by changes in the discount rate. But more or less gradually over the years open-market operations have displaced the discount rate as the more important policy instrument. Today the Federal Reserve Board continues to use discount-rate changes as a part of monetary policy though it places primary reliance on the purchase or sale of government securities in the open market. My proposal would drop the discount rate entirely as an instrument of monetary policy so that sharp changes in discount rates would cease to be disruptive influence in the financial community. But more important the focus on open-market operations would give the Reserve Board a positive, easily modulated, and nondisruptive control over the money supply.

The third constructive institutional change which the Board itself could make has to do with *relative* interest rates and the external balance of payments.

Between World War II and the concordat in 1953 Federal Reserve action was dominated by the "bills-only" policy. The institutional change made by the concordat was important. With the bills-only policy, the purchase of government securities by the Reserve banks in creating reserves was largely limited to short-term issues. This tended to keep interest rates on short terms low *relative* to the rates on longer terms. With the change in policy, somewhat longer-term issues were purchased so that the differential between short-term and long-term issues was reduced. More recently there has been a further shift aimed at the balance-of-payments problem. This has been carried to the point where short-term rates are in approximate balance with long term rates.

But this makes only minor use of the Board's power to influence the relation between short and longer rates. At the end of 1964, the Federal Reserve banks had $37 billion of government securities in their portfolios, yet only $2 billion were in securities having a maturity of five years or more and less than $14 billion had a maturity of one to five years. Well over half the combined portfolio was in short terms and less than 6 per cent in what might properly be called long terms.

The institutional policy which I would recommend is one which would, within the ability of the Board, keep short-term rates well below long terms when our balance of payments was strongly favorable and well above long-term rates when our balance of payments is strongly adverse as it is today.

Look at the problem this way. If we are to have full employment, a stable price level within our country, and stable exchange rates, important unbalances in our external payments are bound to occur whether there is a world shortage of dollars as there was following World War II or a world surplus of dollars as at present. Low short-term rates compared to the short-term rates in other countries will lead to the holding of short-term funds abroad. Relatively high rates here will draw short-term funds here. Such shifting of funds between international centers can help to offset temporary unbalances arising from other sources.

Of course, when we are incurring a deficit in payments, it would be desirable *solely from the viewpoint of payment balance* that all interest rates should be high so as to bring foreign funds to these shores. But a high level of interest rates would almost certainly interfere with maintaining full employment within this country. Fortunately, there are other ways to limit the outflow of long-term capital even though long-term rates are low within the country. On the other hand, movements in short-term funds are much more difficult to influence except through short-term interest rates. Also short-term rates have relatively minor influence on business-investment policy compared to long-term rates. It is therefore feasible to have major swings in short-term rates relative to long term at the same time that the general level of rates is that corresponding to full employment within the country. The policy would thus be consistent with the policy of letting the *level* of interest rates be determined by market forces.

There are two major characteristics of such a policy which should be kept in mind. First, it might from time to time involve costs to both the Treasury and the Reserve banks since, in pursuit of this policy, the Reserve banks might have to buy long terms at high prices and when the balance of payments shifted, sell them at lower prices. Likewise, the Treasury might at times have to pay more for short-term money though other times it might pay less. Such costs could be regarded as a necessary part of good monetary policy and as a relatively inexpensive method of dealing with a temporary unbalance in payments.

The second characteristic of such a policy is that it would not provide a permanent corrective to an unbalance in payments. It can lengthen the period of time in which other forces and other measures can provide a corrective. And this is in itself a valuable contribution, but is not a permanent solution. There is a more fundamental problem here. It may well be that long-run stability in exchange rates between countries is incompatible with full employment and a stable price level within each country.

The three changes in institutional policies I have outlined—a focus on supplying just the amount of money which the public would choose to hold at full employment, a more positive control over the money supply through higher reserve requirements and a higher discount rate, and wider swings in short-term rates relative to long through shifts in Reserve bank portfolios—could all be made by the Federal Reserve Board without legislation and could result in more effective monetary policy.

SIMPLE LEGISLATIVE CHANGES

Monetary policy could be made still more effective if five simple changes were made in the Federal Reserve Act.

The first, and I believe psychologically the most important, legislative change that needs to be made is to revise the preamble to the Act. Its present statement of the chief operating purpose of the Act is obsolete. I am sure it would not occur to the members of the Board to focus their operating activity on the provision of Federal Reserve notes and the rediscounting of commercial paper. These are the least of their concerns. The purpose of Federal Reserve policy has radically changed and the preamble to the Act should be revised to take account of this change. It should indicate the purpose "to bring about a supply of money adequate but not more than adequate to support full employment."

The second legislative change is to establish clearly the authority and responsibility of the Federal Reserve Board over monetary policy. At the present time, the Federal Reserve Board does not by itself have the power to carry out the monetary policy I suggest. By the 1933 amendment to the Act, Congress created a Federal Open Market Committee consisting of the seven members of the Federal Reserve Board and five members elected by directors of the Federal Reserve banks and made it solely responsible for open-market operations which were to be "governed with a view to accommodating

commerce and business and with regard to their bearing upon the
general credit situation of the country." As long as the Federal Reserve System was regarded primarily as a cooperative mutual-aid
enterprise among member banks, with the objective of accommodating commerce and business, this arrangement combining the members of the Board to represent the Federal Government and representatives of the member banks made some sense. But the positive
function of controlling the supply of money is solely a government
function, as the Constitution clearly indicates, and should not be
delegated. The Commission on Money and Credit, in its recent report, recommended that open-market policy should be the sole responsibility of the Federal Reserve Board itself. Until such a change
is made the logic of monetary policy is thoroughly distorted.

A third desirable change is to place the control over discount rates
solely in the hands of the Reserve Board. As long as discount rates
were expected to influence the current markets for credit, there was
logic in having rates determined in part by the regional banks in the
light of local credit conditions. But with discounting an exceptional
action at a rate well above current market rates, full control should
lie with the Reserve Board.

A fourth legislative change has to do with Treasury balances. At
the present time, the Treasury keeps a part of its cash balance on
deposit with private banks and a part on deposit with the Federal
Reserve banks. Every time the Treasury shifts funds from private
bank to Reserve banks, it reduces the reserves available to member
banks; and every time it shifts funds from the Reserve banks to private banks directly or through spending, it increases the reserves
available to member banks. This is, in essence, a form of open-
market operation under the control of the Treasury though in practice
the Treasury works with the Board. But policy now tends to be one
of neutralizing the effect of such changes. Yet the shifting of a part of
the Treasury balances between Reserve and private banks could be a
very easy way to help control short-run fluctuations in the quantity of
reserves called for by monetary policy. The Treasury needs deposits
in private banks as a part of its normal operations. But a part of its
cash could equally well be held either in private or in Reserve banks.
I believe that by legislation, power over the location of that excess
should lie with the Federal Reserve Board, not with the Treasury, and
that this power should be used positively to substitute in part for

short-run open-market operations. Presumably, the legislation would leave the amount of cash free of Board control to negotiations between the Board and the Treasury.

The fifth legislative change I would make would complete the elimination of gold as a *specific* monetary reserve. It is appropriate that our money supply should be based on gold. At the present time gold is an effective international commodity with which to adjust final balances in international payments. But the tying up of gold as a specific legal reserve behind Federal Reserve notes conflicts with this purpose. And even more, it confuses both the logic of our monetary system and the logic of the international gold exchange standard. The elimination of this last vestige of the nineteenth-century gold standard would be desirable, though by no means essential.

These five legislative changes would help the Federal Reserve Board to perform its over-riding function of maintaining the supply of money in our economy at the level required for full employment without demand inflation. And at the same time, they would not require any significant amount of readjustment on the part of the member banks. There are undoubtedly other changes that fall in this same simple category—the Commission on Money and Credit has pointed to some of them—but the five I have suggested seem to me the most important for clarifying the logic of monetary policy and empowering the Federal Reserve Board to carry it out.

BASIC LEGISLATIVE CHANGES

The logic and the unity of monetary policy would be still further advanced if legislation were passed which clarified the lines within the banking system itself. Such legislation would require greater adjustment on the part of private banks but would contribute so much to the conduct of monetary policy in the public interest that I believe they should be made.

At the present time, something like a fifth of the demand deposits in this country are held by banks which are not members of the Federal Reserve System. The Commission on Money and Credit has recommended that "all insured commercial banks should be required to become members of the Federal Reserve System."[5] As a practical matter this would bring all but a fraction of 1 per cent of commercial

[5] *Money and Credit,* The Report of the Commission on Money and Credit (Englewood Cliffs, New Jersey: Prentice-Hall, 1961), p. 77.

banks under the regulation of the Reserve Board. But I see no reason why any bank which has the power to create money should not be required to be a member bank or at least to hold reserves in a Federal Reserve bank against its demand deposits. I would recommend such a requirement, not because deposits are insured but because demand deposits subject to check are maintained. This would bring all the money-creating institutions of the country directly into the System and would be consistent with the Constitution, which places the responsibility for money in the federal government. Such a requirement of reserves for all commercial banks would help to clarify the logic of monetary policy and increase the efficiency with which it can be carried out. In its most recent annual report to Congress, the Federal Reserve Board recommended this change.

This would still leave two major sources of confusion in the money system. The first grows out of the fact that, at the present time, a single commercial bank is likely to carry on two quite different functions: creating money and acting as intermediary in the use of savings. Some bankers will even argue that their banks do not create money. But it is now generally recognized that when a bank creates a demand deposit by making a loan it is creating money and that for the most part this is the way our money supply is created.

On the other hand, when a savings bank or a savings and loan association makes a loan, it does not create demand deposits. All it can do is to lend out funds placed with it. When a savings bank makes a loan it provides the funds in the form of currency or through a check on its deposit account with a commercial bank. In either case it is only passing on money that is already in circulation and is a part of the outstanding money supply. Its action does not add to the money supply. Nor does the retirement of a savings-bank loan reduce the outstanding money supply.

But in a commercial bank both the money-creating and the savings-relending functions are combined in a most confusing fashion. When an individual deposits savings in a commercial bank in which he does not have a demand deposit account, the effect is the same as if he had deposited them in a savings bank except for the small extra reserves the receiving bank has to hold. The bank in effect receives a part of the outstanding money supply and relends it without creating additional money in the process, or, more exactly, this is the net effect on the banking system. But when a commercial bank makes a loan or buys securities by creating a demand deposit it is adding to the money supply. In the daily activity of a commercial bank these two actions which are so importantly different for the economy as a whole can hardly be distinguished by the bank itself. It is not at all surprising that some commercial bankers will say that they don't create deposits but only lend out funds deposited with them.

I believe that our money system will never be intelligible to the intelligent layman and we will never be able to have the statistical material necessary for a close control of our money supply until the two commercial banking functions of money creation and savings-reinvestment are legally separated.

At first thought this may sound like a drastic proposal. But I believe it could be accomplished with very little readjustment in banking arrangements, and with actual benefit to the commercial banks. What I am proposing is that each commercial bank should divide itself into two *legal* entities, one concerned only with demand deposits, the other concerned only with saving and time deposits. These two legal entities could continue to operate as a single enterprise, using the same premises and the same personnel and having the same ownership. And from the point of view of the bank's customers there would appear to be no significant change. But one important difference would result, the separate legal ownership of the loan and investment portfolio. Those loans and investments which were the basis of demand deposits would be legally segregated from those which arose from lending out savings.

From the point of view of monetary policy the most important effect of such a legal separation would be that the Federal Reserve Board could more easily focus on demand deposits and the loans and investments associated with them. In bank reports, the assets back of demand-deposit liabilities would be reported separately and the reserves back of demand deposits would be legally separate from the reserves back of time and savings deposits. The whole effect of the legal separation would be clarifying because it would separate out the monetary aspects of banking and leave the savings-reinvestment function to be put in the same class with and regulated like other savings and loan institutions which do not require the same kind of control because they do not create money.

From the point of view of the commercial banks, the legal separation of demand-deposit function would have at least one great value. It would allow the savings aspect of their present activity to be put on the same regulatory basis as that of other savings institutions with which they are in competition. The Commission on Money and Credit has recognized the disadvantage under which the savings departments of commercial banks now operate and has recommended that the legal requirement that reserves be held in the Federal Reserve bank against their savings and time deposits be eliminated. So long as the demand and saving functions are scrambled in the same institution and with a common portfolio, this proposal seems to me most unwise. But if the two functions were legally separate, there is no reason for special reserve requirements for commercial savings not applicable to other savings institutions and there would be a net gain in the clarity of monetary policy if the reserves in the Federal Reserve banks were limited to reserves on demand deposits.

The very real gain to commercial banks that would come from the elimination of such reserves could also be used to ease the transition to separate legal entities. For example, legislation might be passed which provided that for a period of, say, five years, any member bank which carried out an appropriate legal separation of its monetary and savings functions would not be required to hold a legal reserve with a Reserve bank against its time and savings deposits provided they were covered by federal insurance. Of course, the legislation would also provide that at the end of the transition period all money-creating banks would have to separate this function legally from other functions.

Also, the release of the reserves now held against time and savings deposits would make less burdensome the raising of legal reserve requirements on demand deposits which I suggested earlier.

The other major confusion in our monetary system requiring fundamental legislation is the difference in the way the money supply is expanded, depending on whether the expansion is in the form of currency or in the form of demand deposits. With no change in gold stocks, a given expansion of money in the form of currency requires more than six times as large an open market operation as does an equal expansion in the form of demand deposits.

In the old days of the gold standard, when changes in the supply of gold controlled the money supply, it was appropriate that the reserves back of currency should differ from those back of demand deposits. But today when the main function of reserves in the Federal Reserve banks is for controlling the supply of money outstanding, it would increase the logic of the system and help in the conduct of monetary policy if the two were put on the same basis. There are several ways in which this could be done and I will not go into them here. But so long as the Reserve Board has to engage in open-market operations simply to take account of the public's desire to shift a part of its money holdings from currency into demand deposits or the reverse, the logic of the system will remain confused. The form in which the public chooses to hold its money—currency or demand deposits—should be a matter of indifference to monetary policy. To bring this about would require basic legislation.

Again, there may be other major legislative changes that would be desirable but I believe the three I have suggested are sufficient to give a logically clear and an institutionally effective system for sound monetary policy.

Let me summarize the general argument of my paper.

(1) First, money has a direct effect on aggregate demand and therefore monetary policy is a powerful instrument for raising or reducing aggregate demand and should be the chief instrument for maintaining that level of aggregate demand necessary and just necessary for full employment.

(2) If this function is made the chief objective of monetary policy, there are the three specific institutional changes I have outlined which lie within the power of the Federal Reserve Board and which could both clarify this function and make its performance more effective: The shift from a focus on credit to a focus on the money supply; A more positive control over the money supply; And the greater use of the composition of the Reserve bank portfolios to affect the relation between short- and long-term interest rates.

(3) Then there are the five simple legislative provisions that would contribute to more effective monetary policy: A clear statement of the monetary function in the preamble of the Federal Reserve Act; A provision to re-establish the Federal Reserve Board's authority over monetary policy by giving it sole control over open-market operations; A provision that the Board should have sole control over discount rates; A provision giving the Board the power to determine the location as between private banks and Reserve banks of Federal Treasury deposits in excess of those required in commercial banks for current operations; And a provision to eliminate gold as a specific backing for Federal Reserve notes.

(4) Finally, there are the three major changes which would require that all banks carrying demand deposits subject to check should

be members of the Federal Reserve System; that their money-creating activity be made legally separate from their savings-investment activity; and that expansion of currency should involve the same magnitude of open-market operation as the expansion of demand deposits.

I believe that if these institutional changes were made and our visitor from Mars were then to return, he would have to report back to his constituents that we had a remarkably fine monetary system in this country.

INDEX

adjustment, institutional: pragmatic or instrumental response to, 3–4, 17; progressive approach to, 6; resistance to, 8, 61, 80–82; reasons for, 15, 63–64; in Anglo-America, 17, 22–25, 29–34, 38, 72–84, 87–109; theory of, 21, 27–28, 38; in less developed countries, 21, 33–39, 59–60, 61; use of force for, 60; direction of, 63; to speed growth, 74–75; and New Deal, 87; and legislation, 113, 116–117. SEE ALSO institutions

Africa: sovereignty and property in, 36; building of new society in, 37–38, 116

agriculture: and private ownership of land, 30; technical aid given to, 101

Agriculture, Department of: 97–98

airlines: subsidized to carry mail, 102

Alexander, S. S.: 56–57

Algeria: 64

Amendments: the 5th, 33; the 14th, 33, 117; the 13th, 98

American Creed: anchored in the Constitution, 73; as force for change, 73–74

American Economic Republic: 33

American Tobacco Company: 101

Anglo-America: institutions of, 22–34, 38. SEE ALSO United States

Area Redevelopment Act: for public improvements, 107. SEE ALSO New Deal

Asia: sovereignty and property in, 36; building of new society in, 116

Ataturk, Kemal: 36

Australia High Court: institutes adjustment, 117

Bank of the United States: creation of, 91–93; opposition to, 95–96

banks: may create or destroy money, 50–51; and credit, 61; regulation of cash reserves by, 98; during financial crises, 99. SEE ALSO Federal Reserve Bank; Hamilton, Alexander

Barrientos, René: 64

Bentham, Jeremy: on social change, 113

Bergson, Abram: 17

Berk, A. A.: 33

Bernard, Simon: 94

Beveridge, William H., Lord: 146

Board of Engineers for Fortifications, U.S.: 94

Bonn Constitution: on equality between sexes, 114–115

Breitel, Charles D.: on judicial lawmaking, 121

British Town and Country Planning Act: 115

Calhoun, John C.: 93

capitalism: 38

ceremonialism: nature of, 6; contamination by, 12; awesome to the followers, 13. SEE ALSO superstition

change. SEE adjustment, institutional

children, illegitimate: rights of, 120

citizenship: as privilege, 36

Civil Rights Act of 1964: 107–108; and equality of voting, 118

civilization: de-institutionalization of, 8–9, 16

Clayton Act: 101

Coast Survey, U.S.: Jefferson as chief planner of, 92; functions of, 94

Coast and Geodetic Survey: 99

collective bargaining: establishing devices of, 26; and court decisions, 100; and National Labor Relations Board, 106. SEE ALSO New Deal